HAL•LEONARD®
GUITAR PLAY-ALONG

AUDIO ACCESS INCLUDED

EAGLES
ACOUSTIC

PLAYBACK+
Speed • Pitch • Balance • Loop

To access audio, visit:
www.halleonard.com/mylibrary

Enter Code
3814-3394-0895-1351

T0057871

Cover photo courtesy Photofest

ISBN 978-1-4768-1410-0

HAL•LEONARD®

Visit Hal Leonard Online at
www.halleonard.com

Contact us:
Hal Leonard
7777 West Bluemound Road
Milwaukee, WI 53213
Email: info@halleonard.com

In Europe, contact:
Hal Leonard Europe Limited
42 Wigmore Street
Marylebone, London, W1U 2RN
Email: info@halleonardeurope.com

In Australia, contact:
Hal Leonard Australia Pty. Ltd.
4 Lentara Court
Cheltenham, Victoria, 3192 Australia
Email: info@halleonard.com.au

Guitar Notation Legend

THE MUSICAL STAFF shows pitches and rhythms and is divided by bar lines into measures. Pitches are named after the first seven letters of the alphabet.

TABLATURE graphically represents the guitar fingerboard. Each horizontal line represents a string, and each number represents a fret.

4th string, 2nd fret — 1st & 2nd strings open, played together — open D chord

HALF-STEP BEND: Strike the note and bend up 1/2 step.

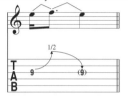

WHOLE-STEP BEND: Strike the note and bend up one step.

GRACE NOTE BEND: Strike the note and immediately bend up as indicated.

SLIGHT (MICROTONE) BEND: Strike the note and bend up 1/4 step.

BEND AND RELEASE: Strike the note and bend up as indicated, then release back to the original note. Only the first note is struck.

PRE-BEND: Bend the note as indicated, then strike it.

VIBRATO: The string is vibrated by rapidly bending and releasing the note with the fretting hand.

PALM MUTING: The note is partially muted by the pick hand lightly touching the string(s) just before the bridge.

HAMMER-ON: Strike the first (lower) note with one finger, then sound the higher note (on the same string) with another finger by fretting it without picking.

PULL-OFF: Place both fingers on the notes to be sounded. Strike the first note and without picking, pull the finger off to sound the second (lower) note.

LEGATO SLIDE: Strike the first note and then slide the same fret-hand finger up or down to the second note. The second note is not struck.

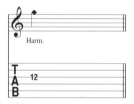

SHIFT SLIDE: Same as legato slide, except the second note is struck.

TRILL: Very rapidly alternate between the notes indicated by continuously hammering on and pulling off.

TAPPING: Hammer ("tap") the fret indicated with the pick-hand index or middle finger and pull off to the note fretted by the fret hand.

NATURAL HARMONIC: Strike the note while the fret-hand lightly touches the string directly over the fret indicated.

PINCH HARMONIC: The note is fretted normally and a harmonic is produced by adding the edge of the thumb or the tip of the index finger of the pick hand to the normal pick attack.

TREMOLO PICKING: The note is picked as rapidly and continuously as possible.

VIBRATO BAR DIVE AND RETURN: The pitch of the note or chord is dropped a specified number of steps (in rhythm), then returned to the original pitch.

VIBRATO BAR SCOOP: Depress the bar just before striking the note, then quickly release the bar.

VIBRATO BAR DIP: Strike the note and then immediately drop a specified number of steps, then release back to the original pitch.

Additional Musical Definitions

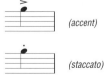

(accent) • Accentuate note (play it louder).

(staccato) • Play the note short.

D.S. al Coda • Go back to the sign (𝄋), then play until the measure marked "***To Coda***," then skip to the section labelled "**Coda**."

D.C. al Fine • Go back to the beginning of the song and play until the measure marked "***Fine***" (end).

Fill • Label used to identify a brief melodic figure which is to be inserted into the arrangement.

N.C. • Harmony is implied.

• Repeat measures between signs.

• When a repeated section has different endings, play the first ending only the first time and the second ending only the second time.

CONTENTS

After the Thrill Is Gone

Words and Music by Don Henley and Glenn Frey

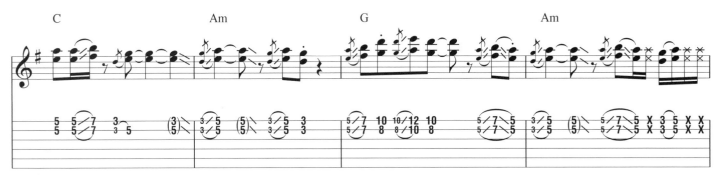

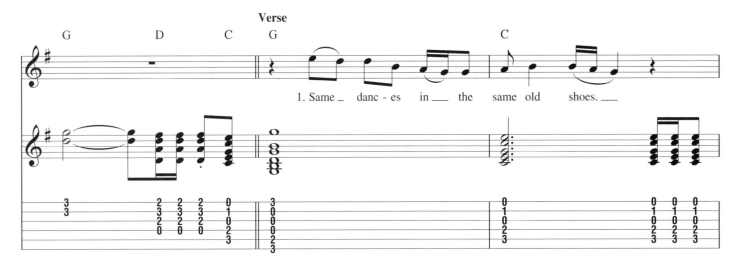

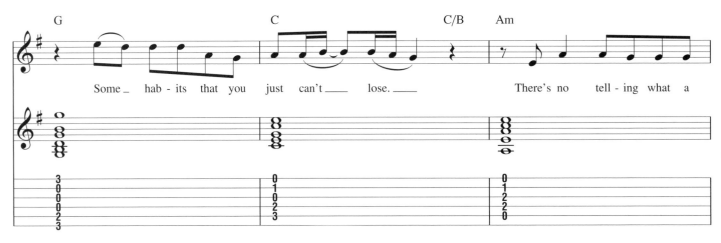

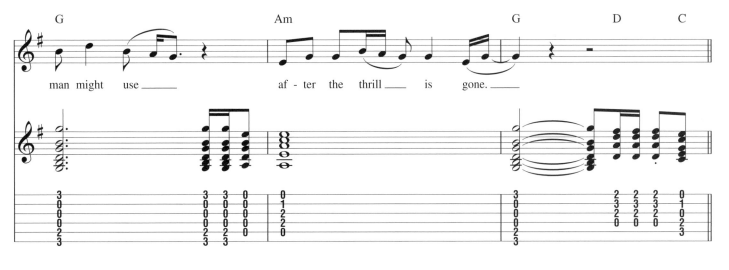

man might use _____ af - ter the thrill _____ is gone. _____

Verse

2. The flame _ ris - es, but it soon de - scends. _ Emp - ty pag - es, and _ a

fro - zen pen. _____ You're not quite lov - ers and you're not quite friends _____

af - ter the thrill _____ is gone, _____ whoa, _____ af - ter the thrill _____ is gone. _

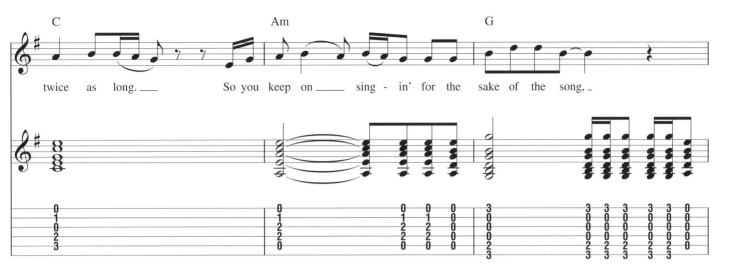

twice as long. ___ So you keep on ___ sing - in' for the sake of the song, ___

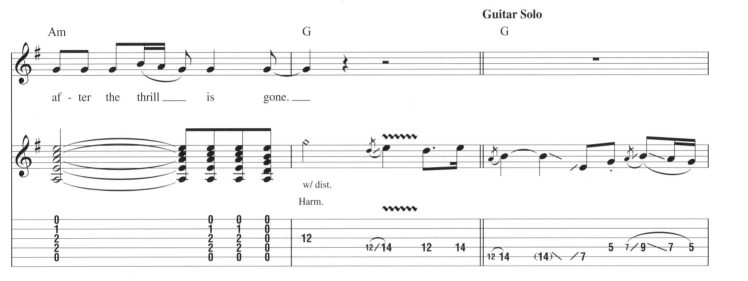

Guitar Solo

af - ter the thrill ___ is gone. ___

w/ dist.
Harm.

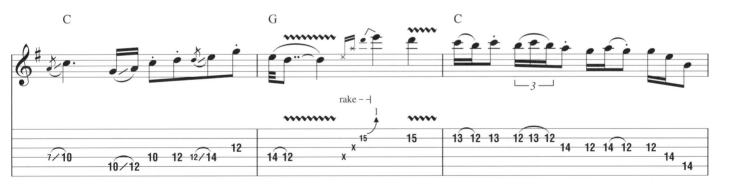

rake

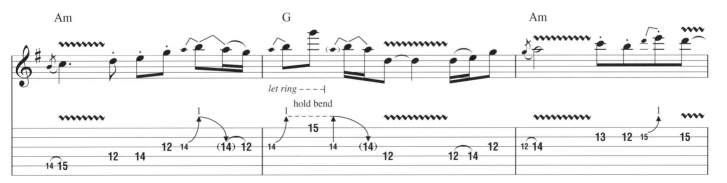

let ring

hold bend

7

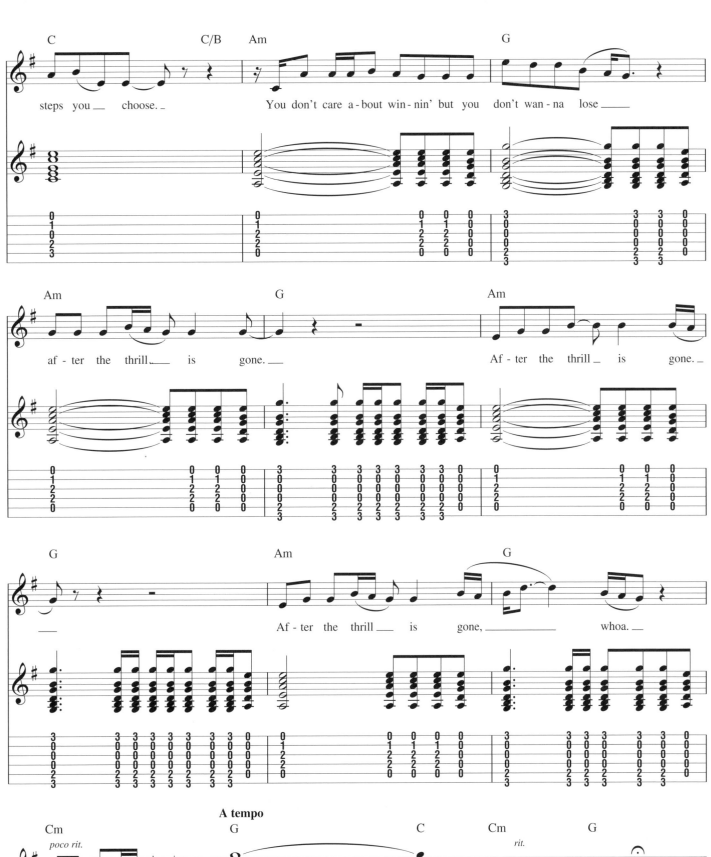

Desperado

Words and Music by Don Henley and Glenn Frey

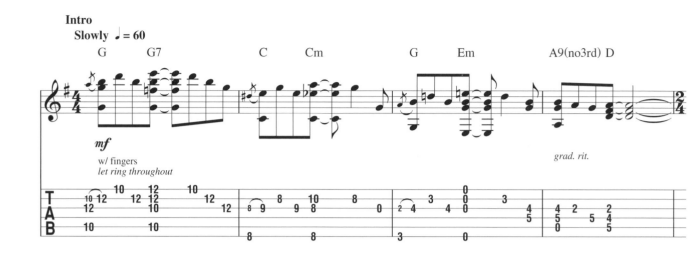

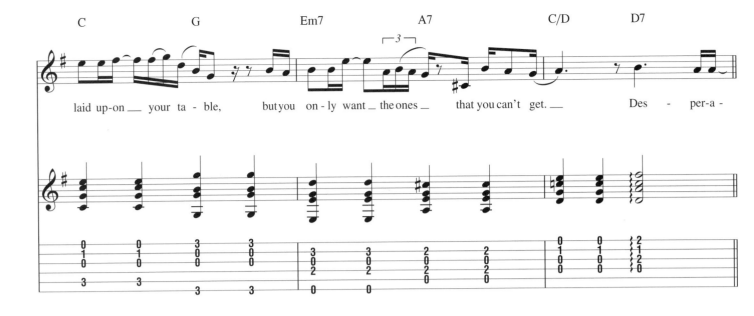

laid up-on your ta - ble, but you on - ly want the ones that you can't get. Des - per-a-

Chorus

- do, oh, you ain't gettin' no young - er. Your

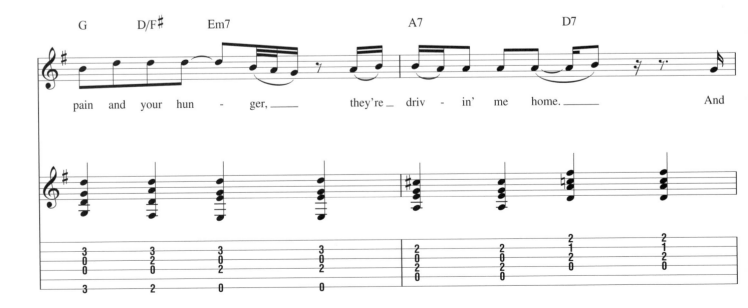

pain and your hun - ger, they're driv - in' me home. And

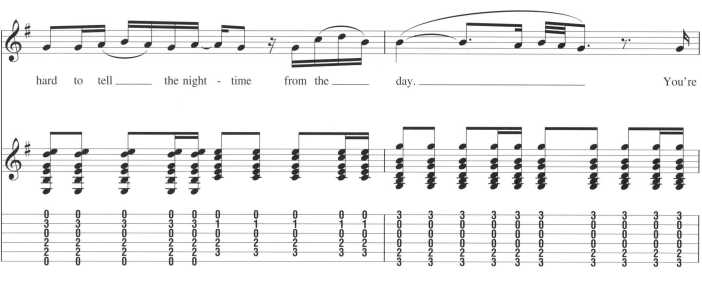

hard to tell _____ the night - time from the _____ day. _____ You're

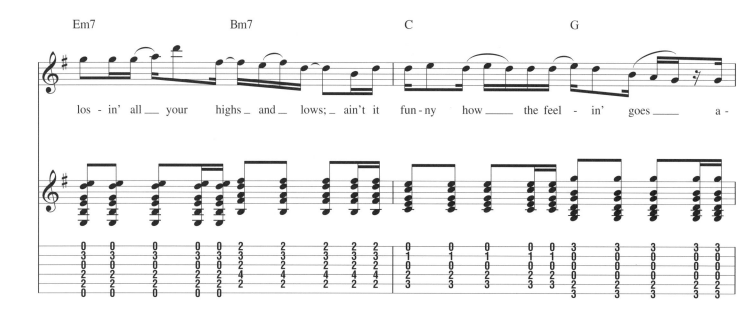

los - in' all __ your highs __ and __ lows; __ ain't it fun - ny how _____ the feel - in' goes _____ a -

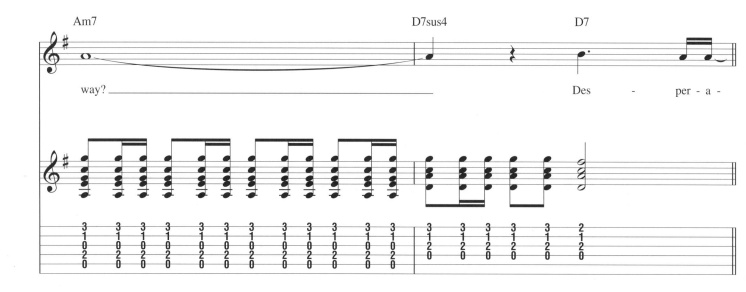

way? _____ Des - per - a -

Chorus

- do, why don't __ you __ come to your sen - ses? Come

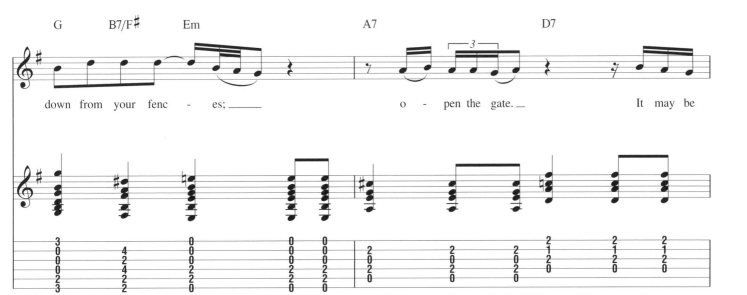

down from your fenc - es; _____ o - pen the gate. __ It may be

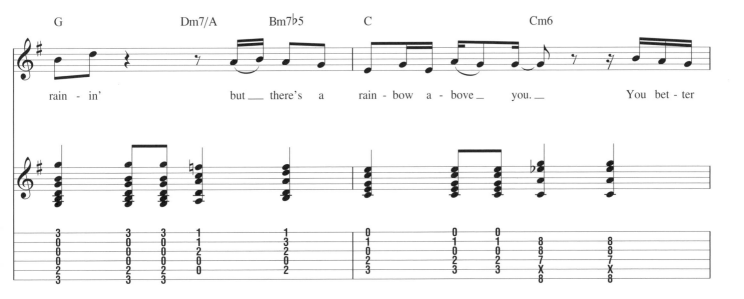

rain - in' but __ there's a rain - bow a - bove __ you. __ You bet - ter

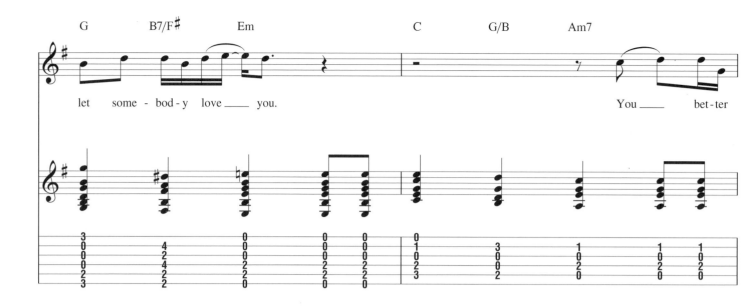

let some-bod-y love _____ you. You _____ bet-ter

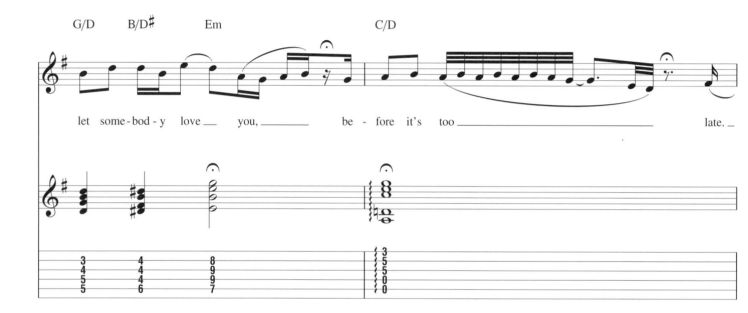

let some-bod-y love _____ you, _____ be - fore it's too _____ late. _

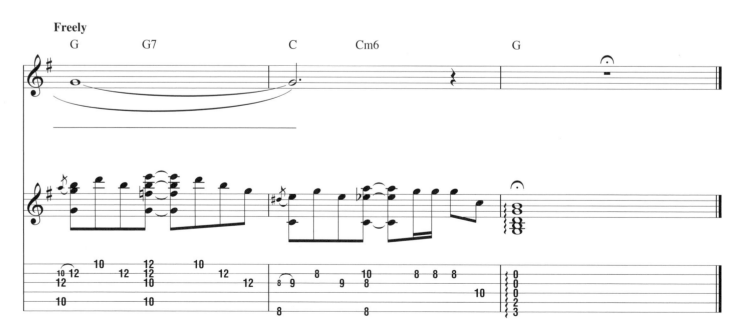

New Kid in Town

Words and Music by John David Souther, Don Henley and Glenn Frey

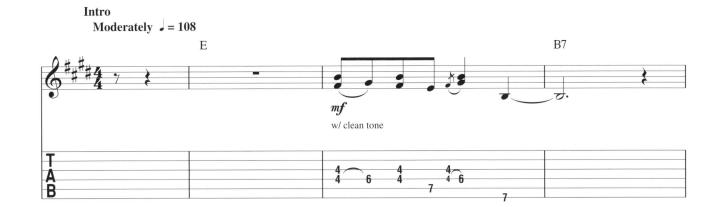

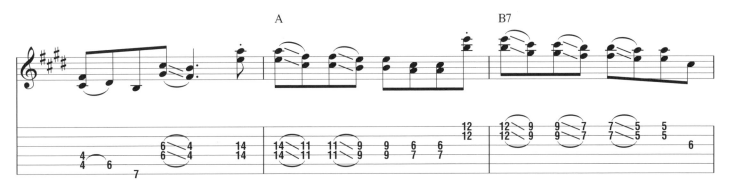

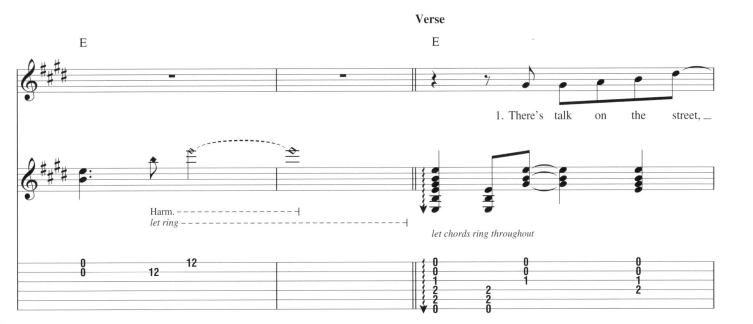

it sounds _ so _ fa - mil - iar.

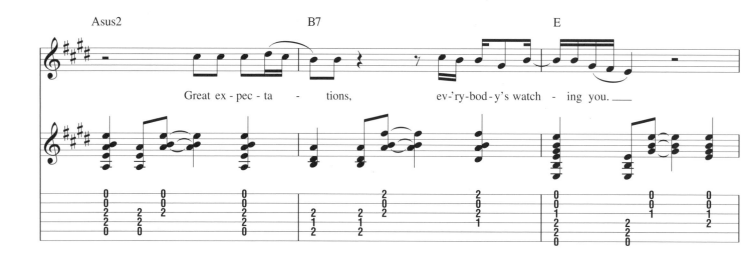

Great ex - pec - ta - tions, ev-'ry-bod-y's watch - ing you. _

Peo - ple you meet, _ they all _ seem _ to know _

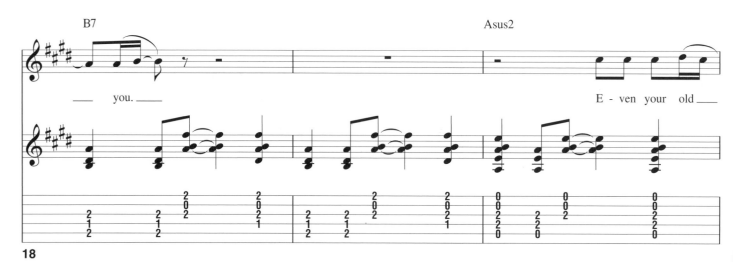

_ you. _ E - ven your old _

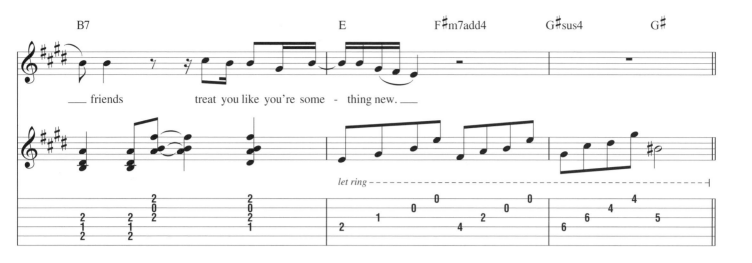

_____ friends treat you like you're some - thing new. _____

Chorus

John - ny come late - ly, the new kid in town.

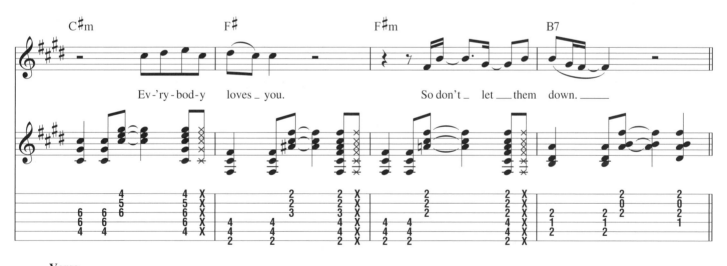

Ev-'ry-bod-y loves _ you. So don't _ let _ them down. _____

Verse

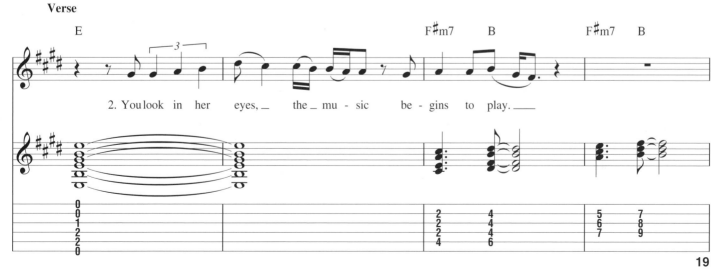

2. You look in her eyes, _ the _ mu - sic be - gins to play. _____

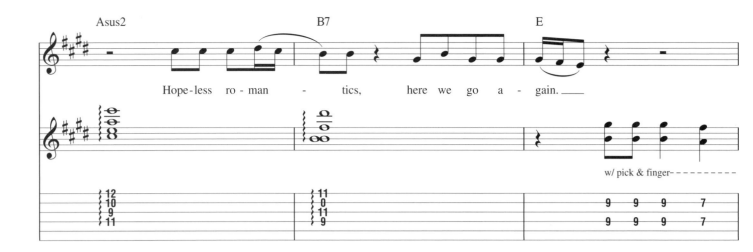

Hope-less ro-man - tics, here we go a - gain.

w/ pick & finger

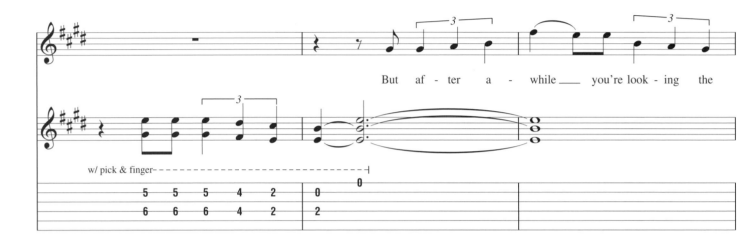

But af - ter a - while you're look - ing the

w/ pick & finger

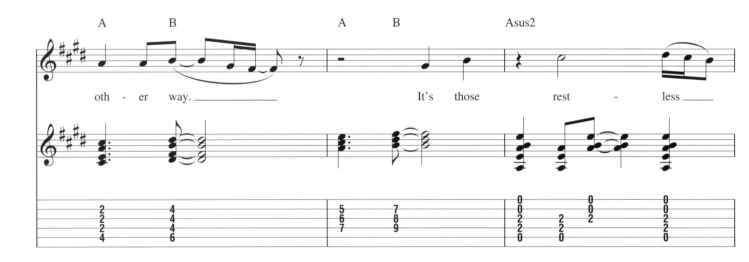

oth - er way. It's those rest - less

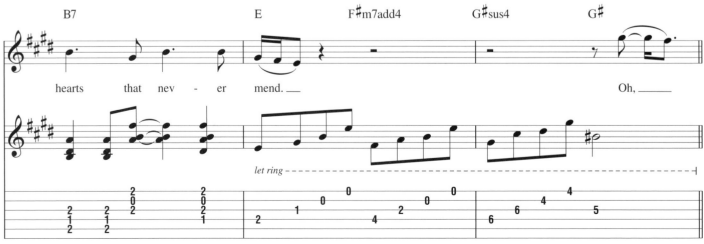

hearts that nev - er mend. Oh,

let ring

Chorus

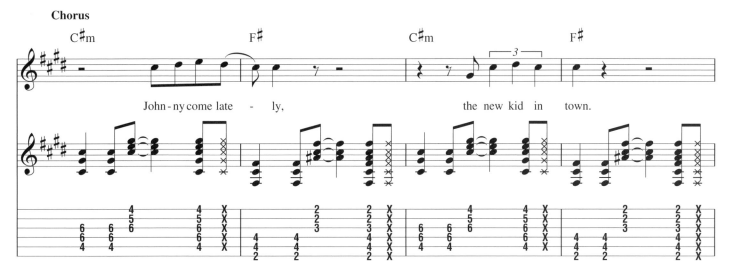

John- ny come late - ly, the new kid in town.

Will she still love _ you when you're not a - round? _____

Guitar Solo

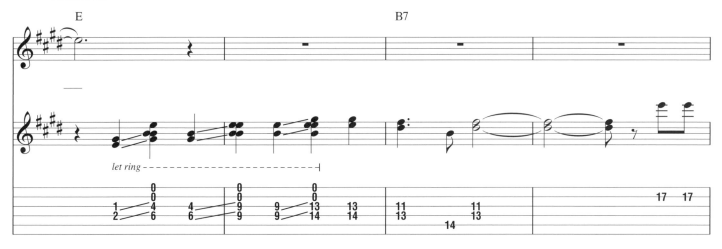

let ring -

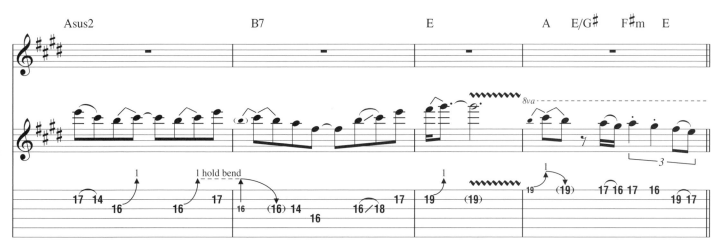

Interlude

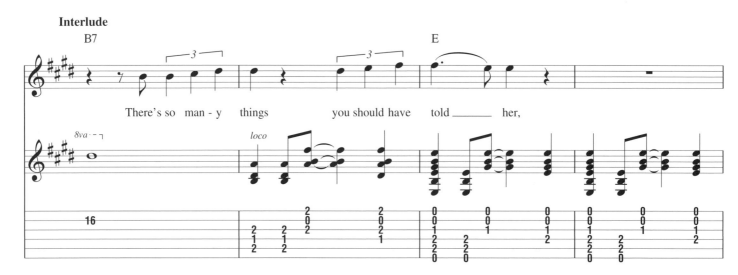

There's so man-y things you should have told ____ her,

but night af-ter night you're will-ing to hold ____ her, just hold ____ her.

Verse

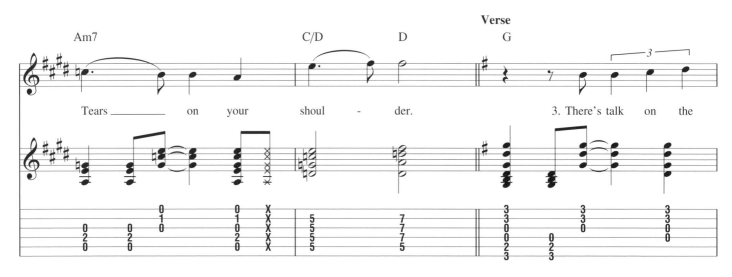

Tears ____ on your shoul - der. 3. There's talk on the

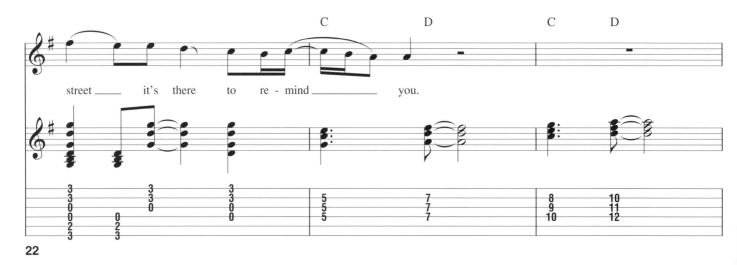

street ____ it's there to re - mind ____ you.

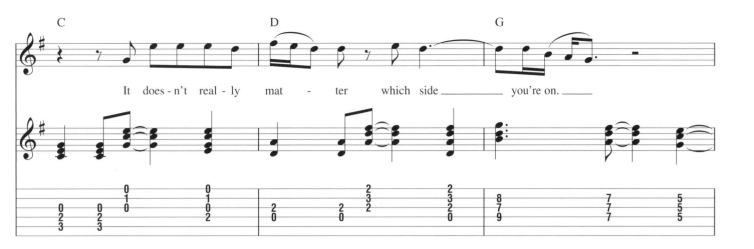

It does-n't real-ly mat-ter which side _____ you're on. _____

You're walk-ing _____ a-way _____ and they're _ talk-ing be-hind _

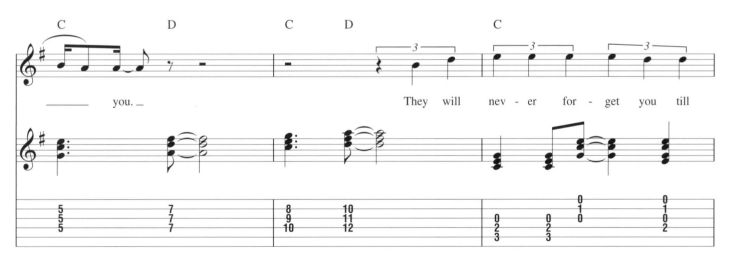

_____ you. _ They will nev-er for-get you till

some-bod-y new comes a-long. _____

Chorus

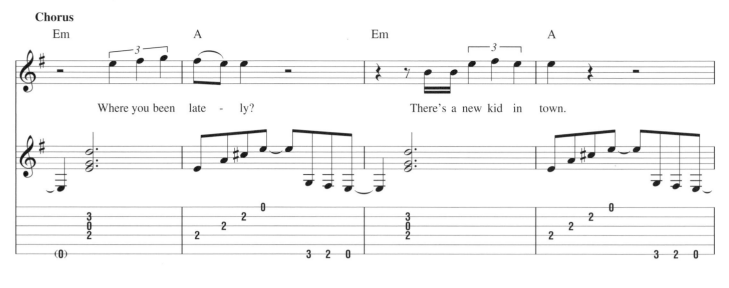

Where you been late - ly? There's a new kid in town.

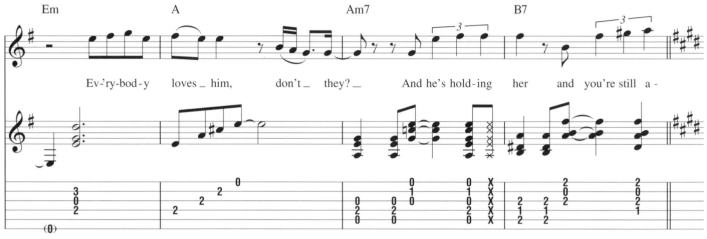

Ev'ry-bod-y loves _ him, don't _ they? _ And he's hold-ing her and you're still a-

Outro

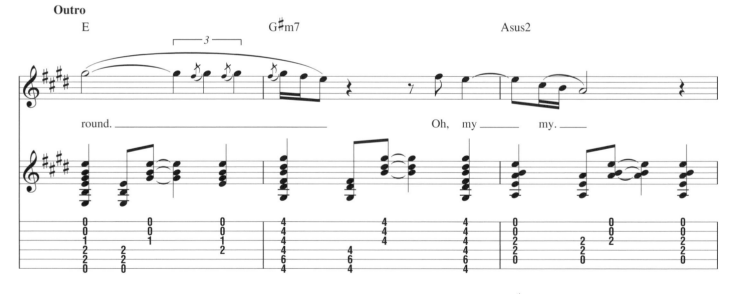

round. _____ Oh, my _____ my. _____

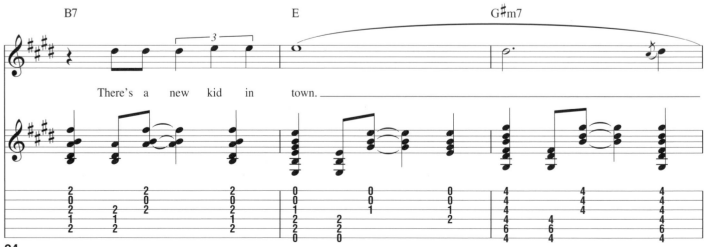

There's a new kid in town. _____

24

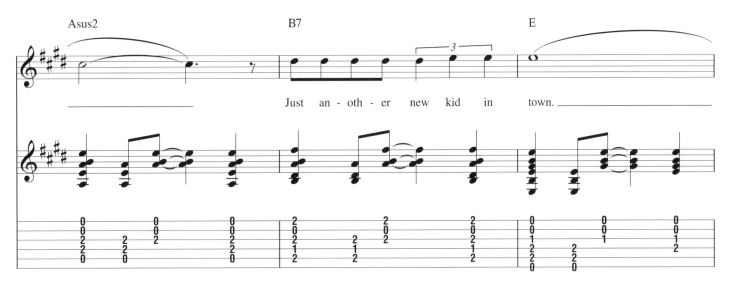

Just an-oth-er new kid in town.

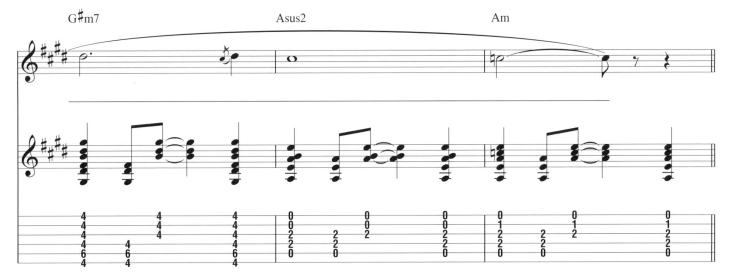

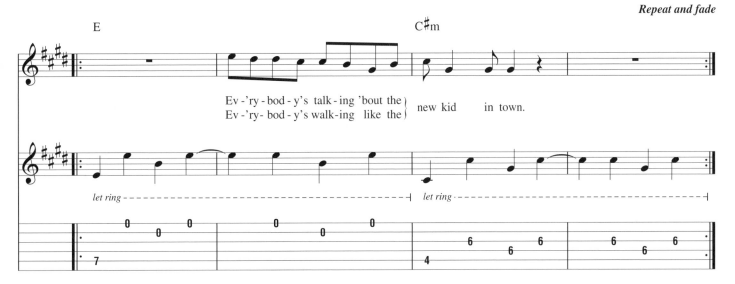

Repeat and fade

Ev-'ry-bod-y's talk-ing 'bout the
Ev-'ry-bod-y's walk-ing like the } new kid in town.

let ring

let ring

Lyin' Eyes

Words and Music by Don Henley and Glenn Frey

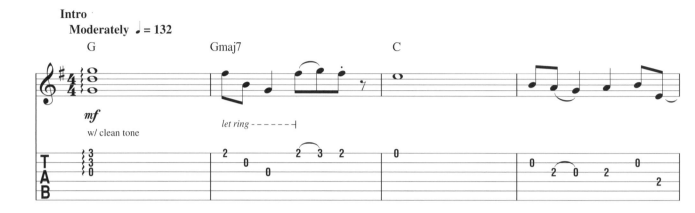

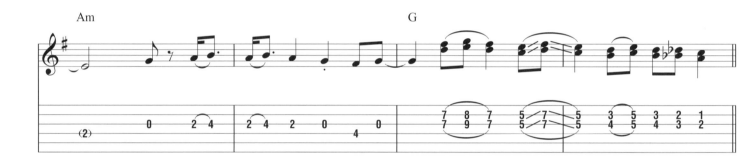

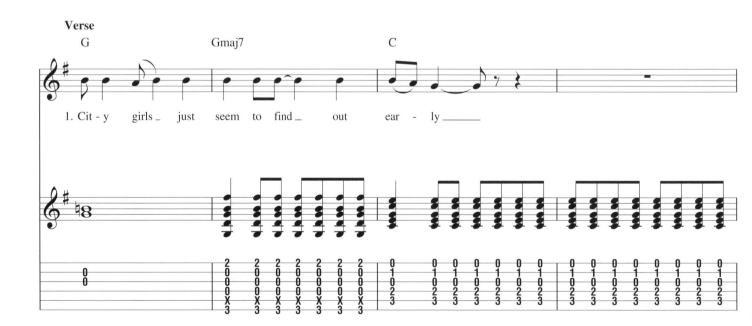

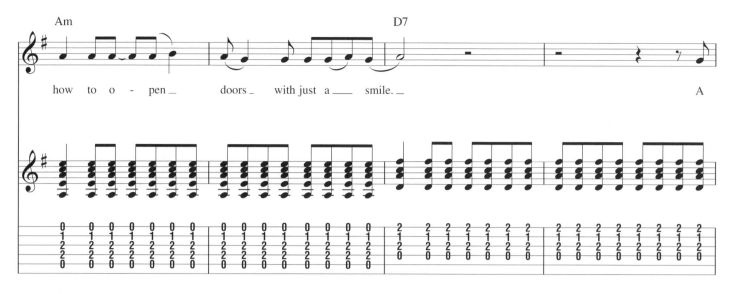

how to o - pen _ doors _ with just a ___ smile. _   A

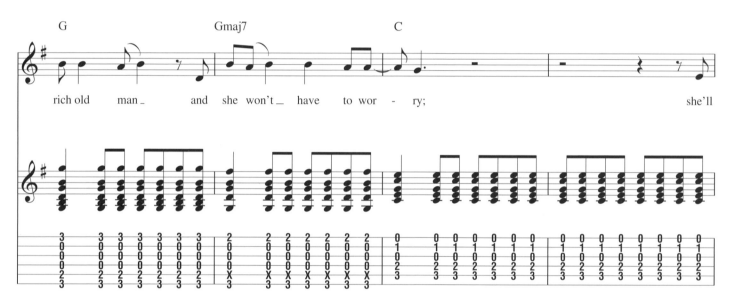

rich old man _ and she won't _ have to wor - ry;   she'll

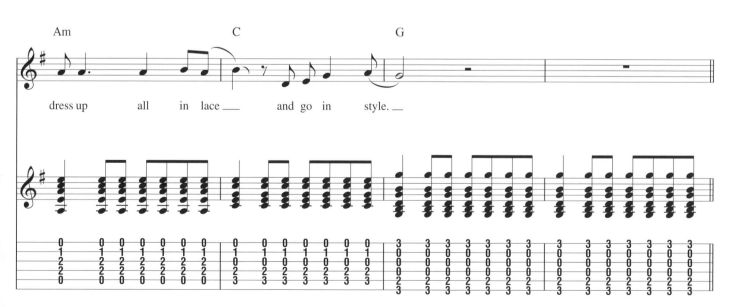

dress up all in lace ___ and go in style. _

Verse

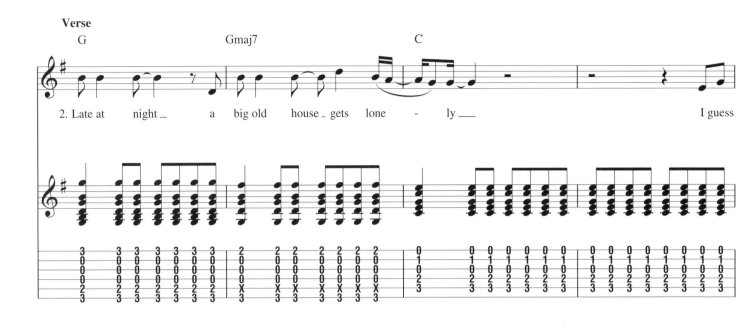

2. Late at night _ a big old house _ gets lone - ly _ I guess

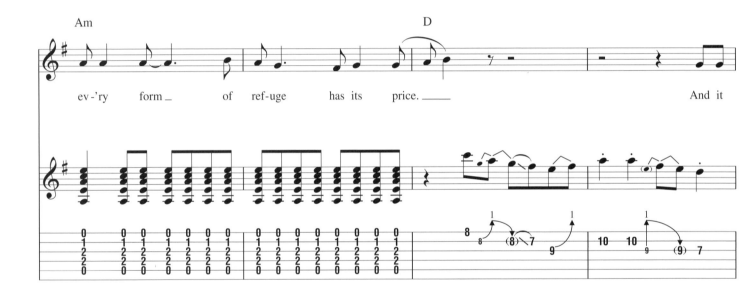

ev -'ry form _ of ref-uge has its price. ____ And it

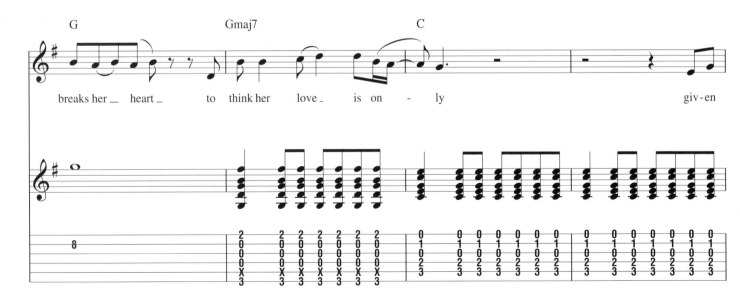

breaks her _ heart _ to think her love _ is on - ly giv-en

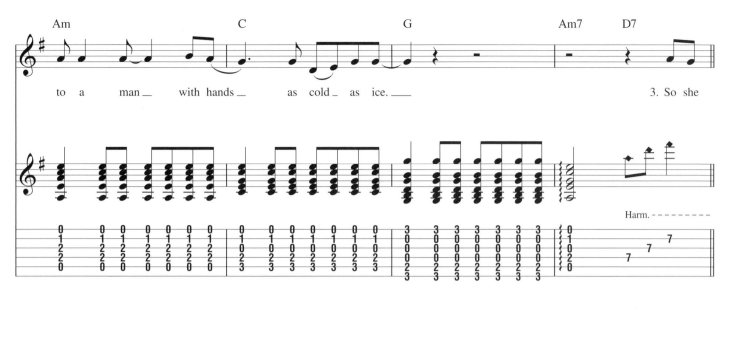

to a man ___ with hands ___ as cold ___ as ice. ___ 3. So she

Verse

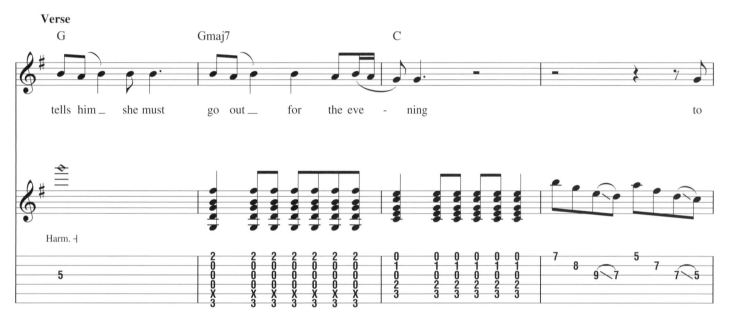

tells him ___ she must go out ___ for the eve - ning to

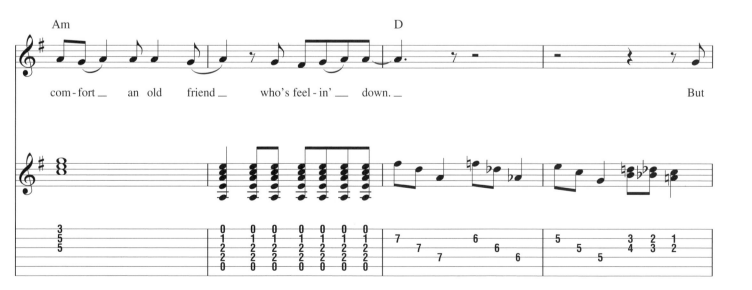

com - fort ___ an old friend ___ who's feel - in' ___ down. ___ But

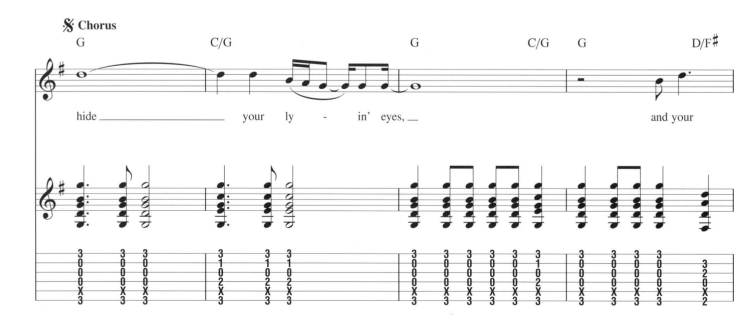

smile _____ is a thin ___ dis - guise.

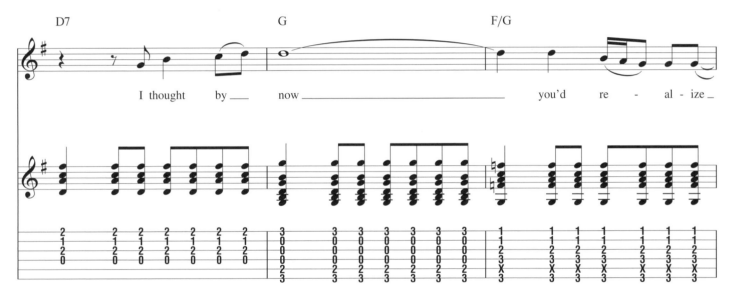

I thought by ___ now _____ you'd re - al - ize ___

To Coda 2

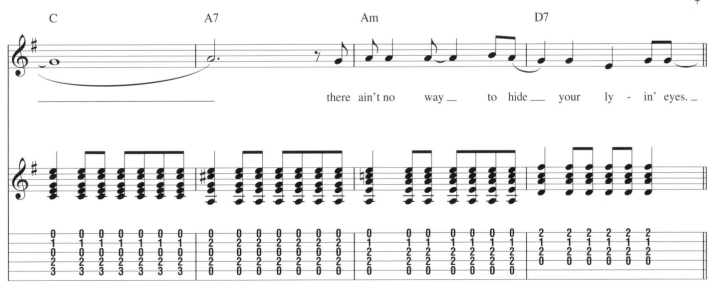

_____ there ain't no way ___ to hide ___ your ly - in' eyes. ___

Interlude

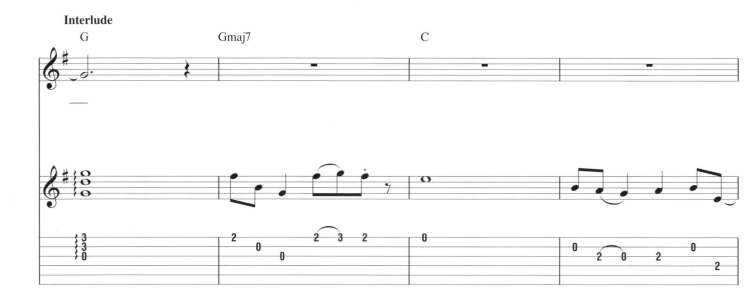

4. On the

Verse

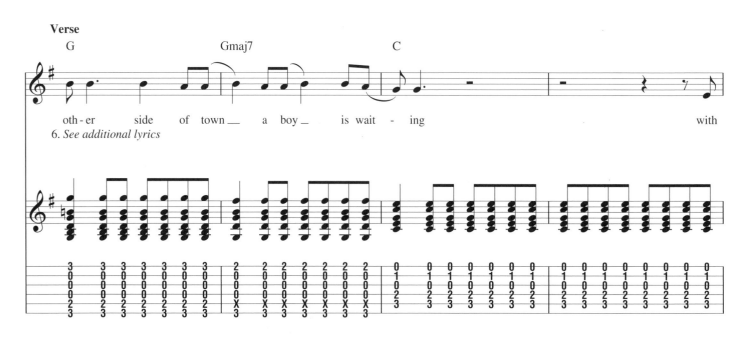

oth - er   side   of   town ___   a boy ___   is wait - ing   with

6. See additional lyrics

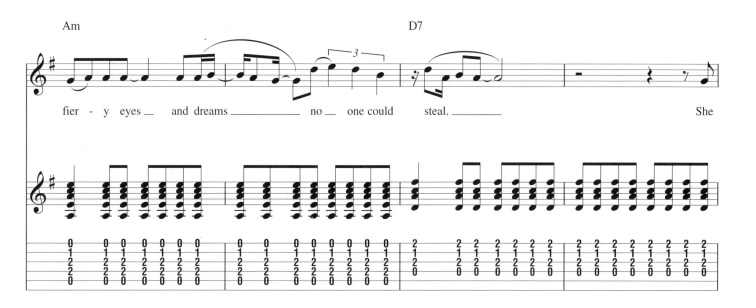

fier - y eyes ___ and dreams _____ no ___ one could steal. _____ She

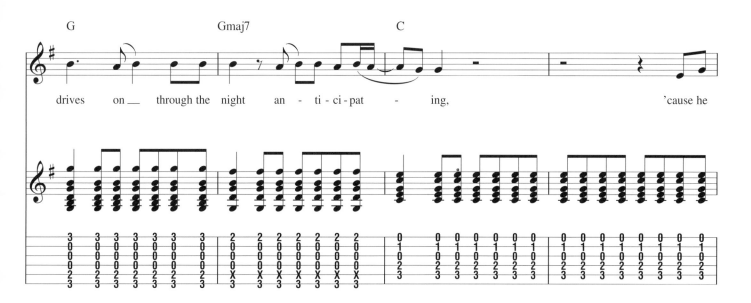

drives on ___ through the night an - ti - ci - pat - ing, 'cause he

To Coda 1

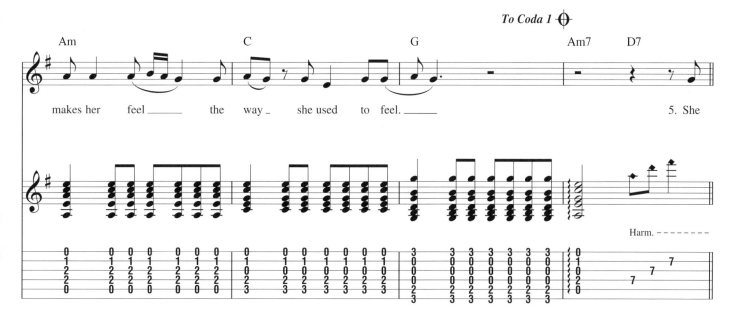

makes her feel _____ the way ___ she used to feel. _____ 5. She

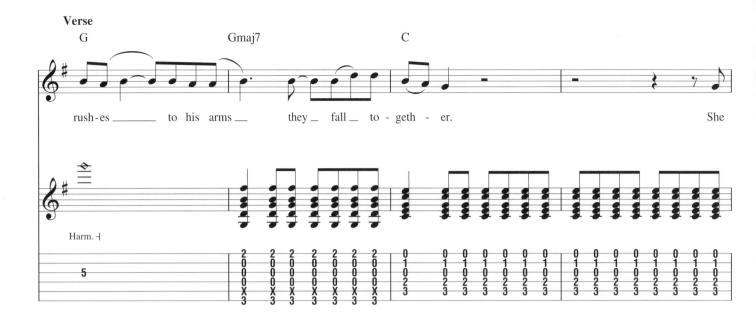

rush-es _____ to his arms ___ they _ fall __ to - geth - er. She

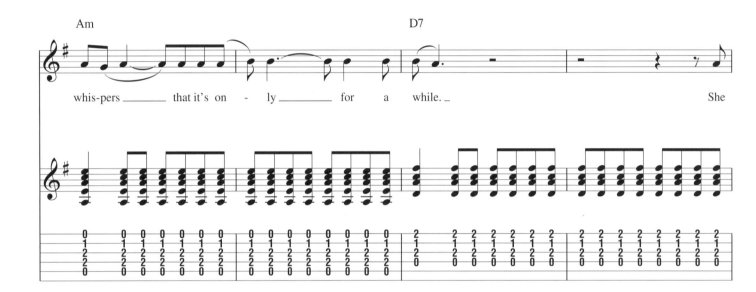

whis-pers _____ that it's on - ly _____ for a while. __ She

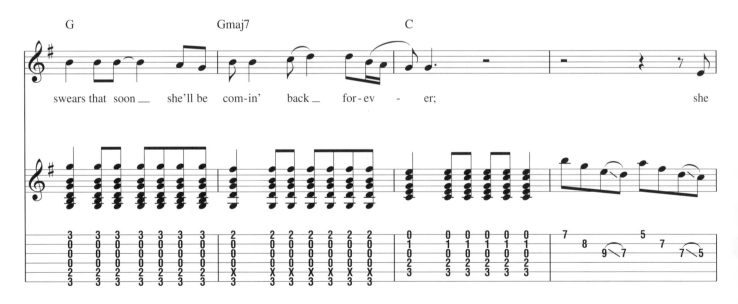

swears that soon ___ she'll be com-in' back __ for - ev - er; she

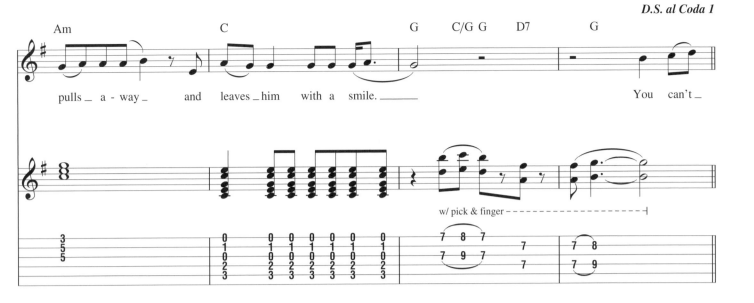

Coda 1

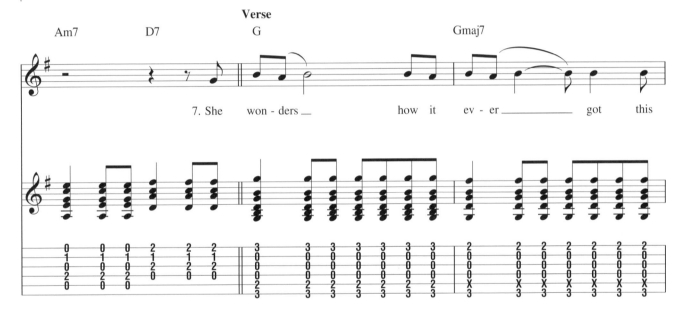

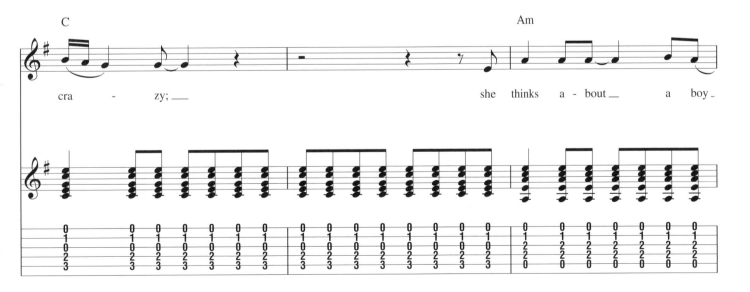

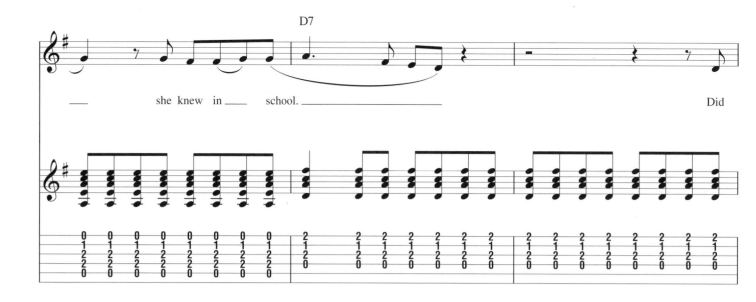

she knew in ___ school. _____ Did

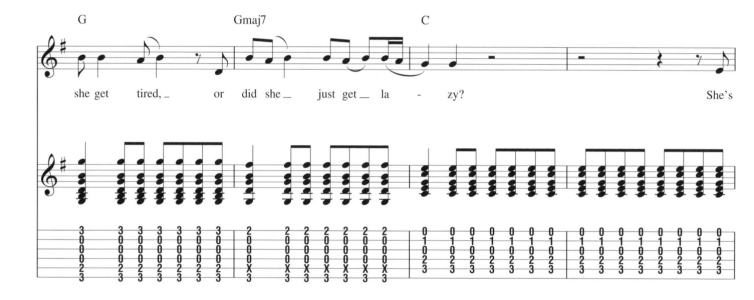

she get tired, _ or did she _ just get _ la - zy? She's

so far gone _ she feels _ just like a fool. _____

Verse

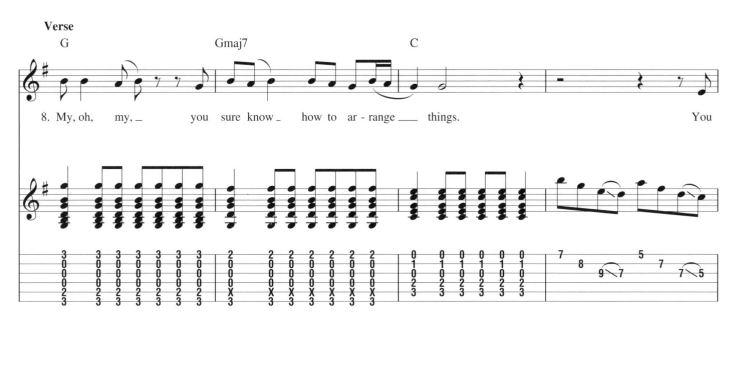

8. My, oh, my, _ you sure know _ how to ar - range _ things. You

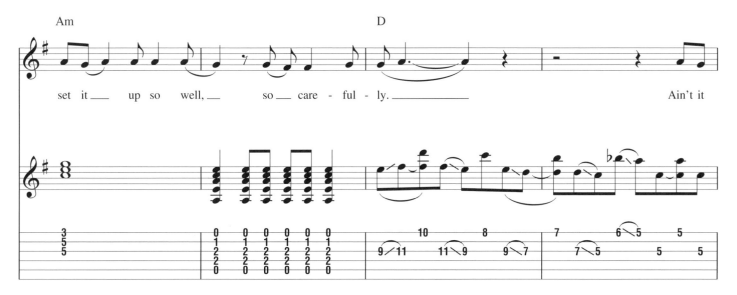

set it _ up so well, _ so _ care - ful - ly. _____ Ain't it

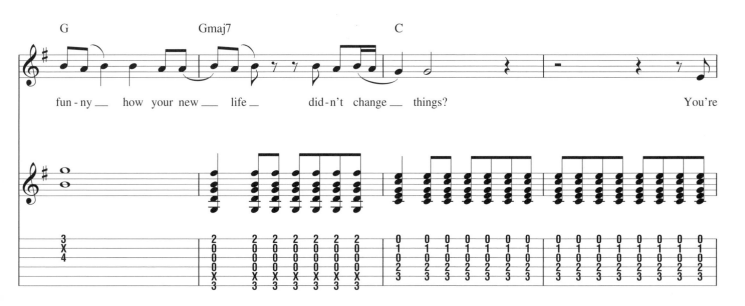

fun - ny _ how your new _ life _ did-n't change _ things? You're

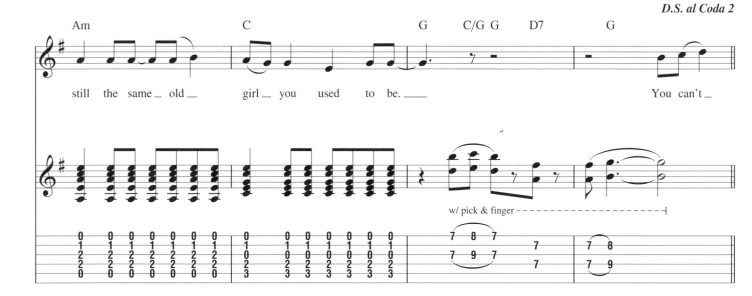

still the same _ old _ girl _ you used to be. _ You can't _

Coda 2

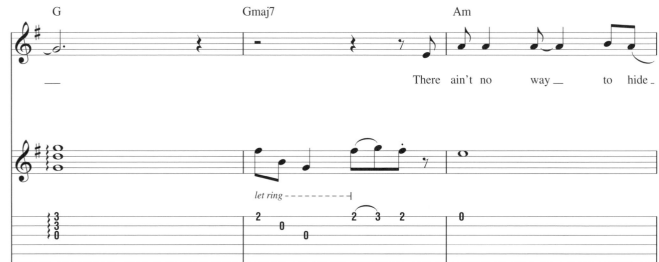

_ There ain't no way _ to hide _

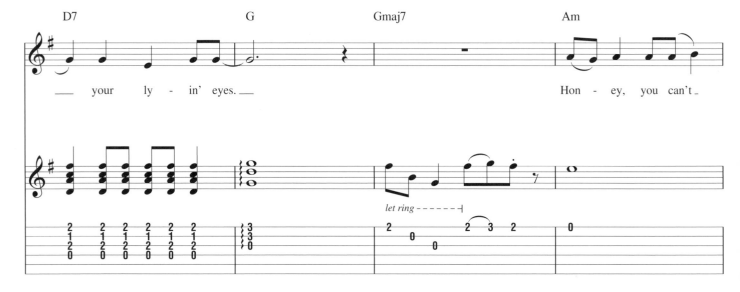

_ your ly - in' eyes. _ Hon - ey, you can't _

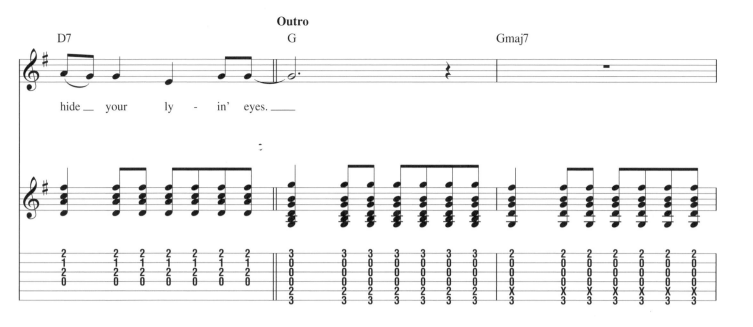

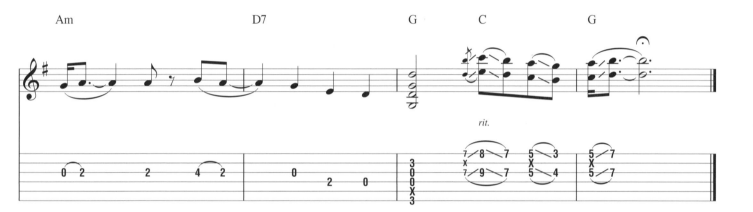

Additional Lyrics

    6. She gets up and pours herself a strong one,
       And stares out at the stars up in the sky.
       Another night; it's gonna be a long one.
       She draws the shade and hangs her head to cry.

Peaceful Easy Feeling

Words and Music by Jack Tempchin

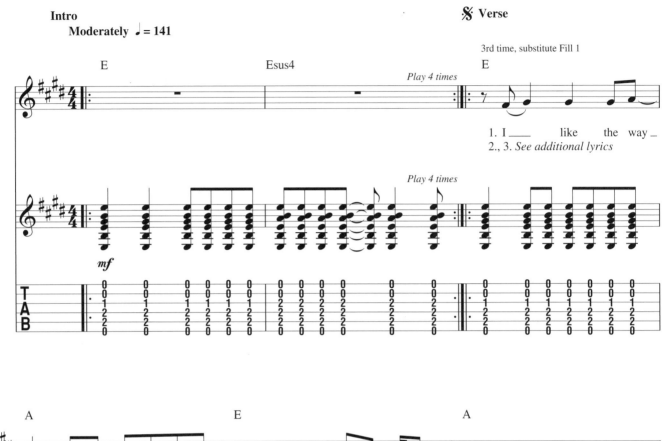

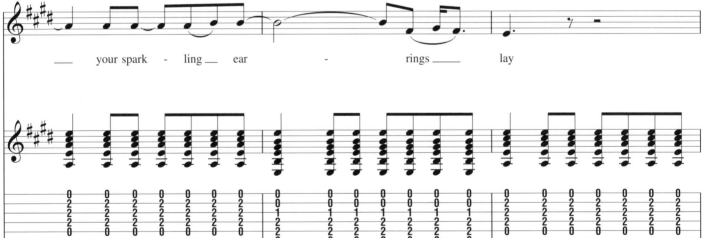

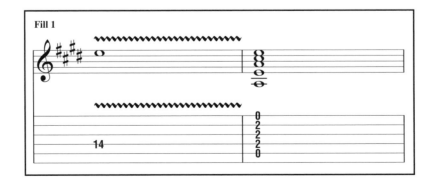

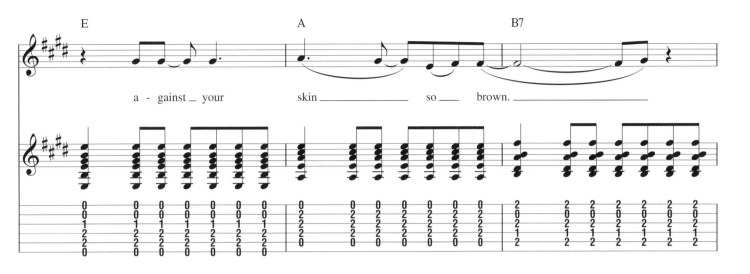

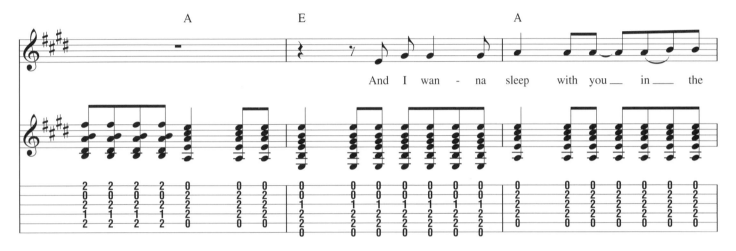

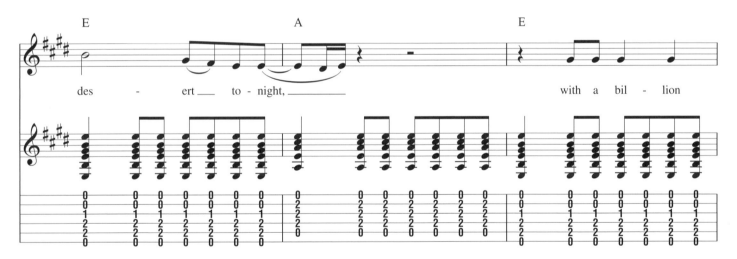

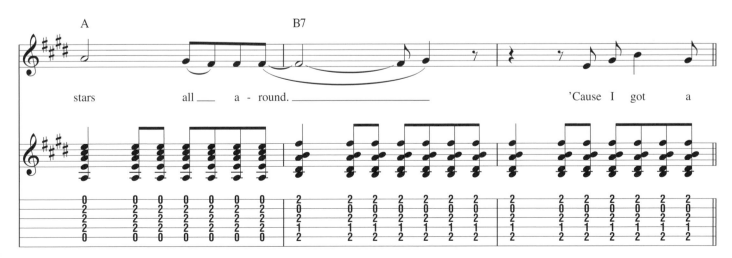

Chorus

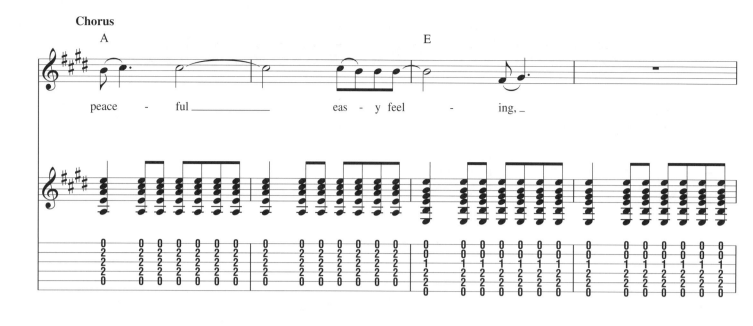

peace - ful _____ eas - y feel - ing, _

and I __ know you won't _ let me __ down, _____ 'cause I'm

To Coda ⊕

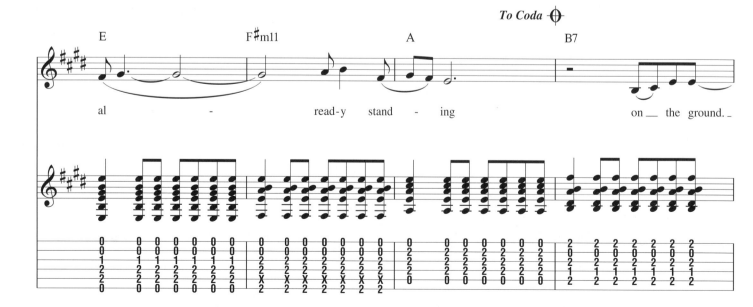

al - read-y stand - ing on __ the ground. _

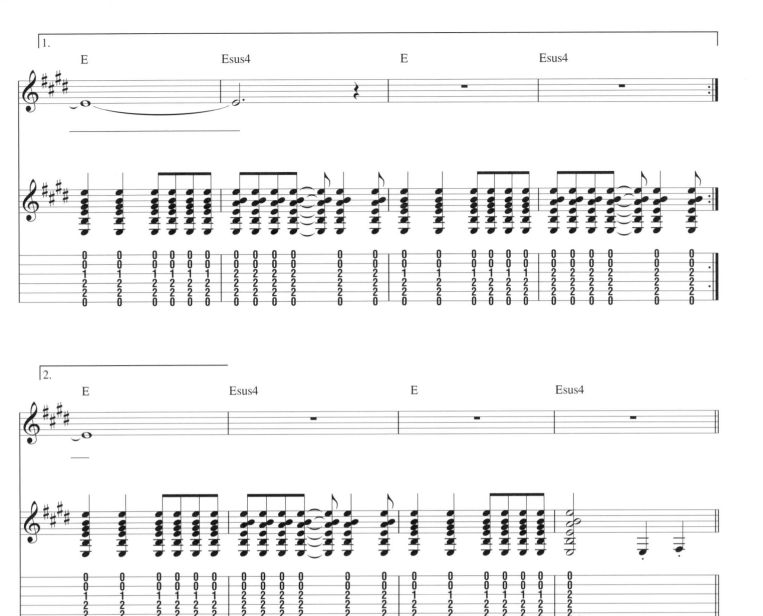

Guitar Solo

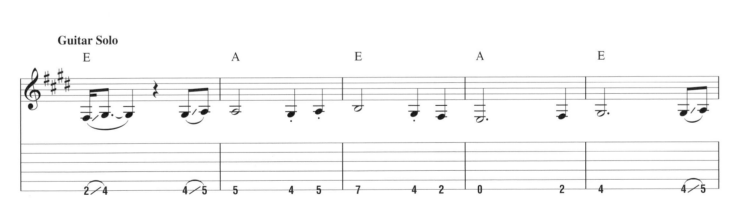

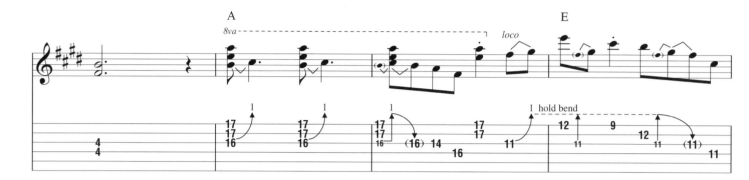

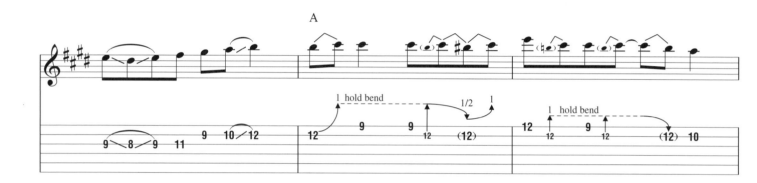

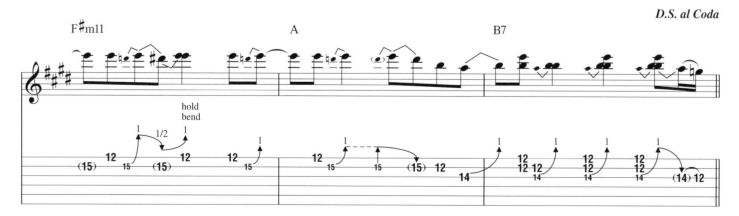

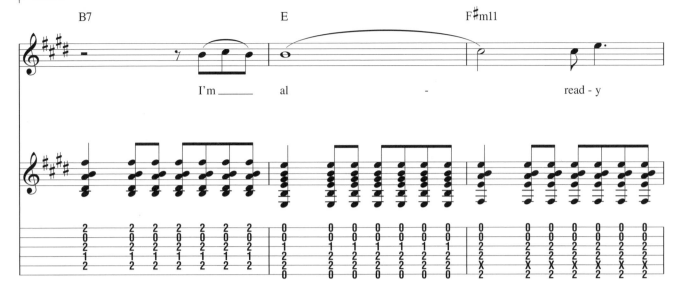

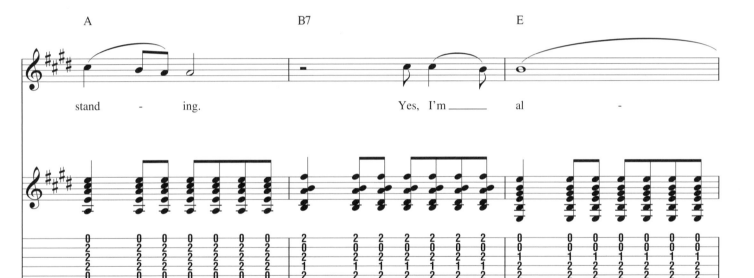

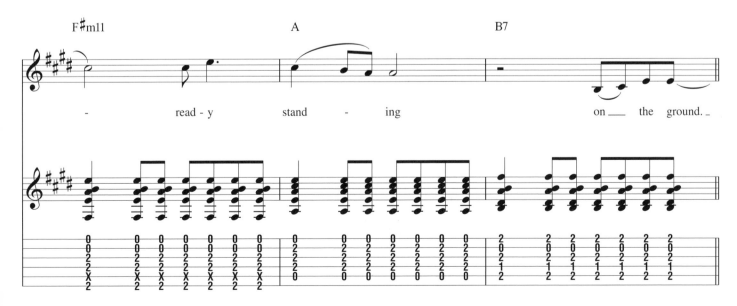

Outro

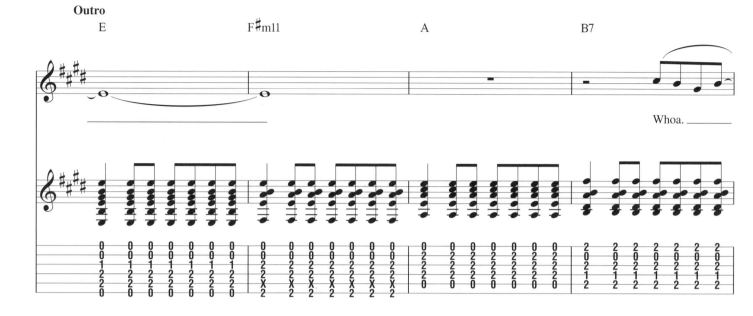

Whoa. _____

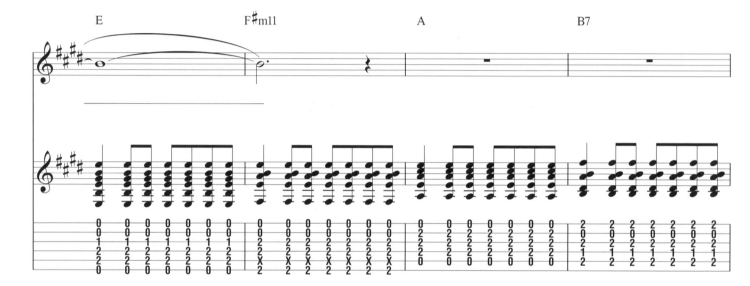

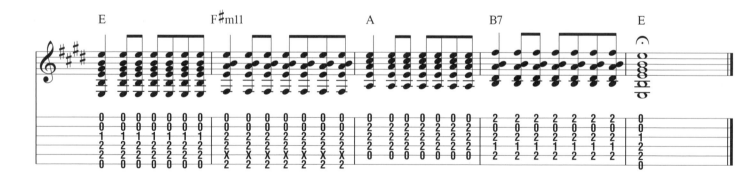

Additional Lyrics

2. And I found out a long time ago
   What a woman can do to your soul.
   Aw, but she can't take you anyway;
   You don't already know how to go.
   And I got a...

3. I get this feeling I may know you
   As a lover and a friend.
   But this voice keeps whispering in my other ear,
   Tells me I may never see you again.
   'Cause I get a...

The Sad Café

Words and Music by Don Henley, Glenn Frey, Joe Walsh and John David Souther

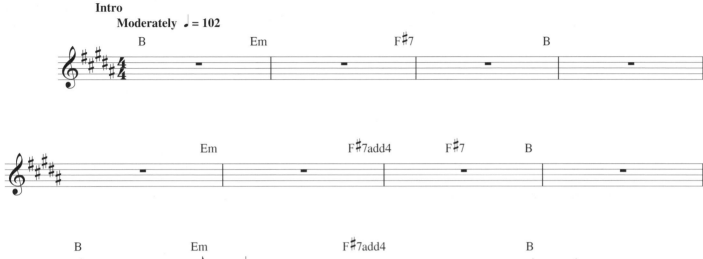

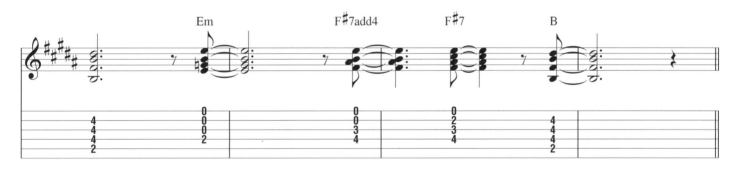

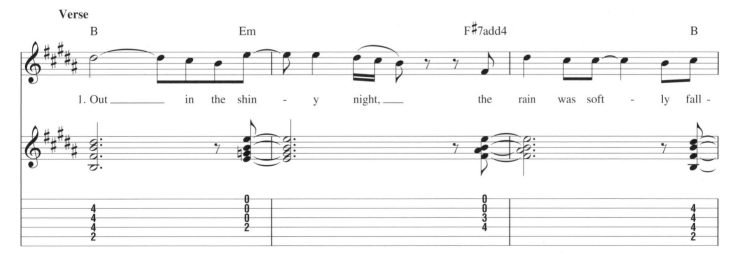

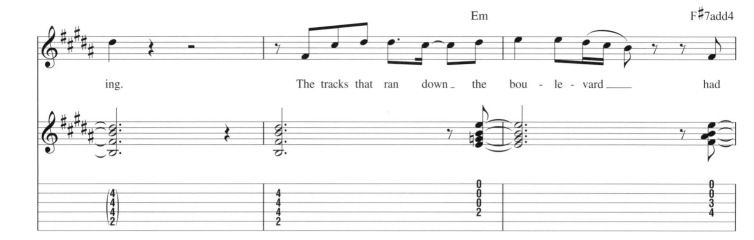

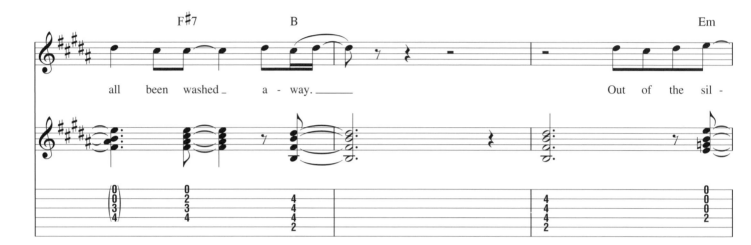

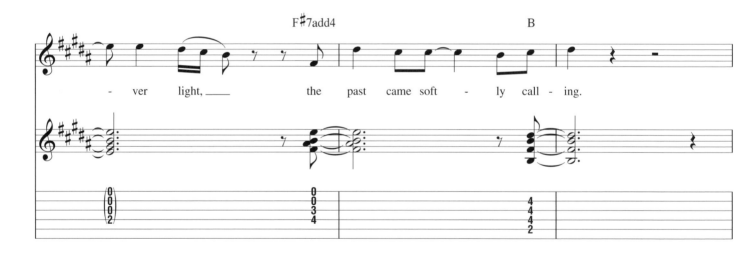

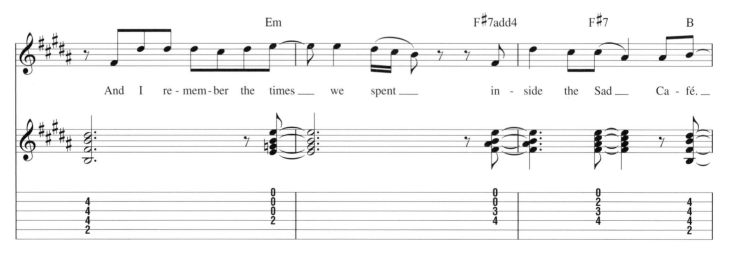

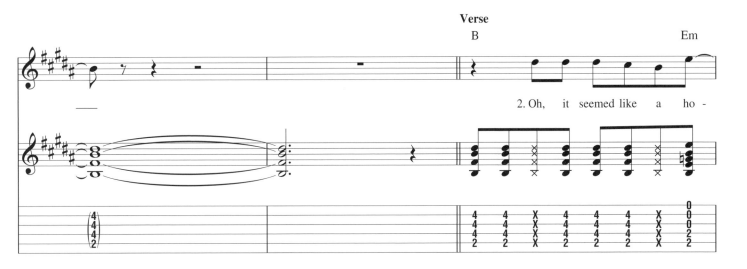

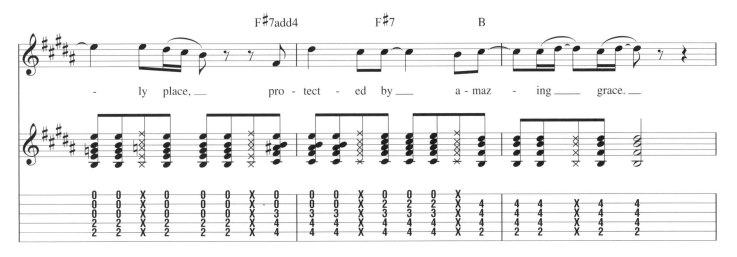

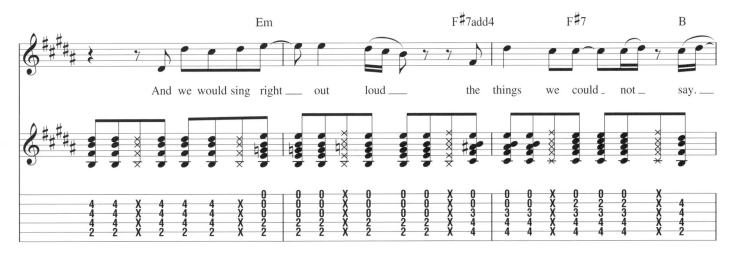

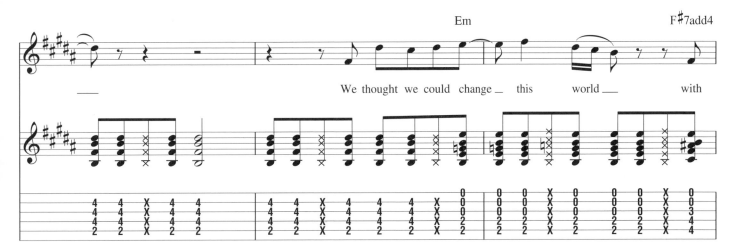

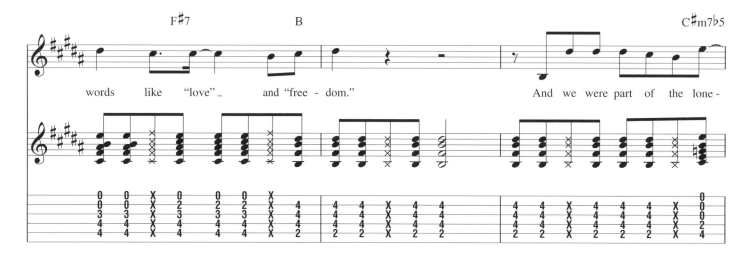

words like "love" and "free - dom." And we were part of the lone -

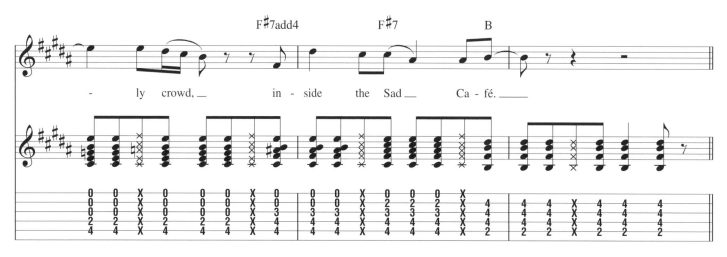

- ly crowd, in - side the Sad Ca - fé.

Bridge

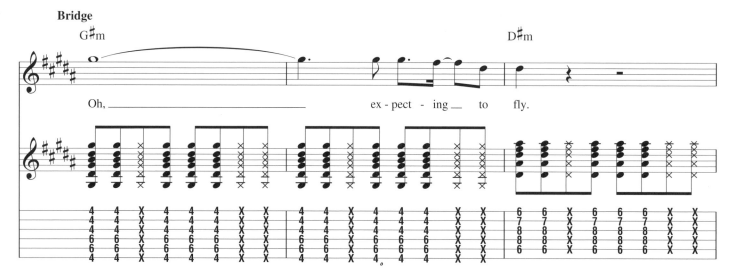

Oh, _____ ex - pect - ing _ to fly.

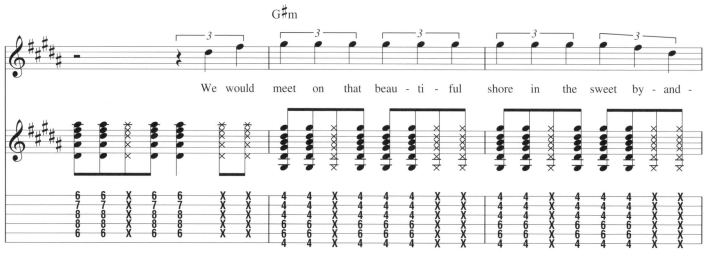

We would meet on that beau - ti - ful shore in the sweet by - and -

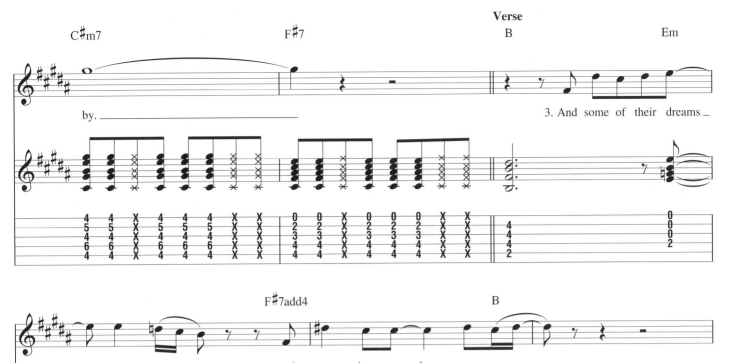

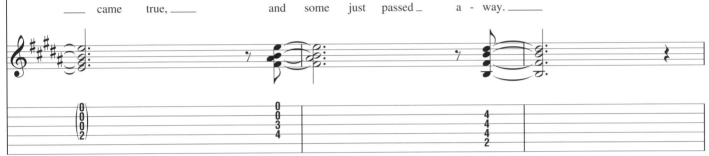

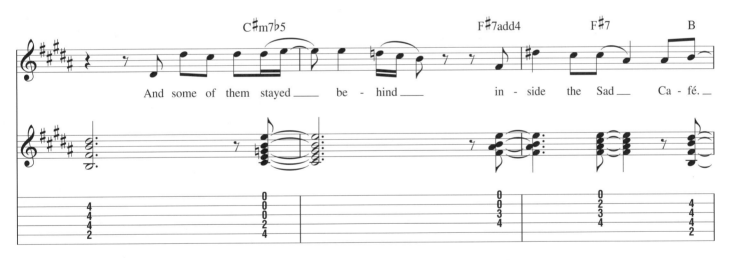

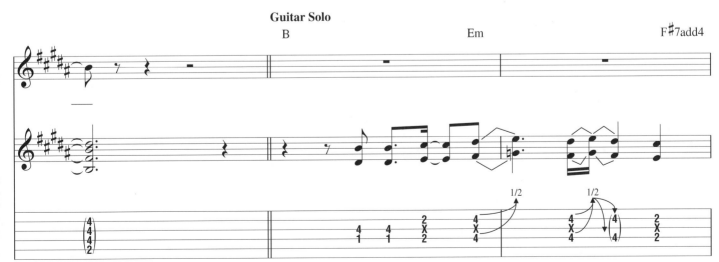

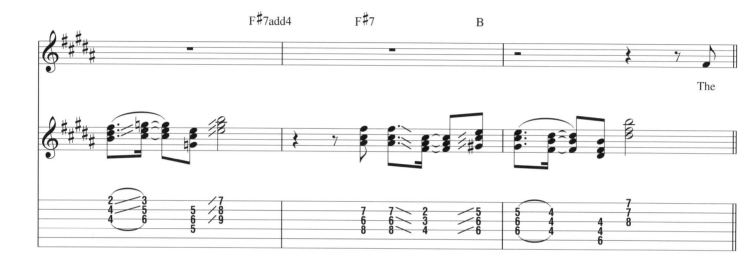

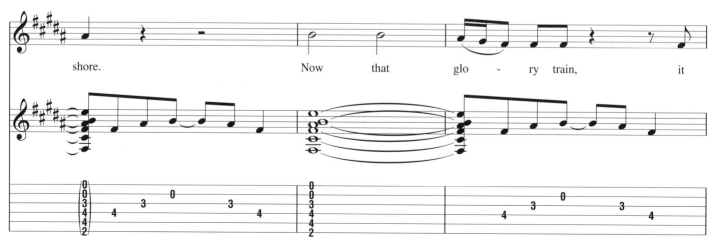

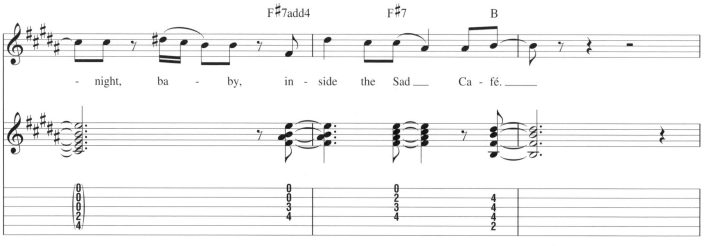

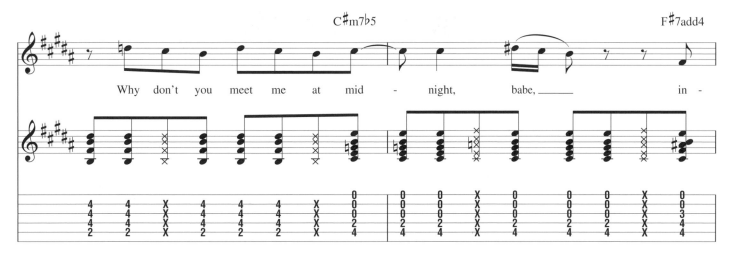

C#m7b5 · F#7add4

Why don't you meet me at mid - night, babe, _____ in -

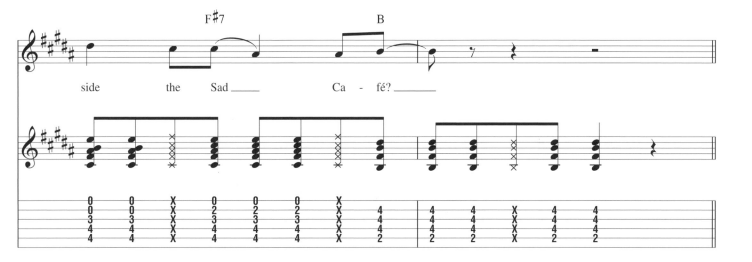

F#7 · B

side the Sad _____ Ca - fé? _____

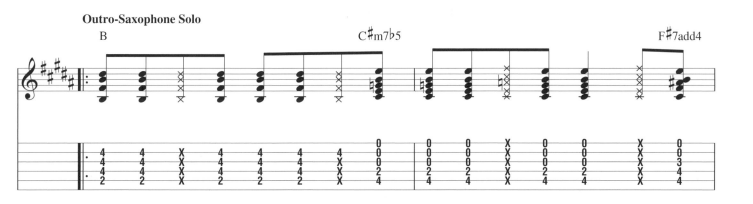

Outro-Saxophone Solo

B · C#m7b5 · · · · · · · · · · · · · · F#7add4

Repeat and fade

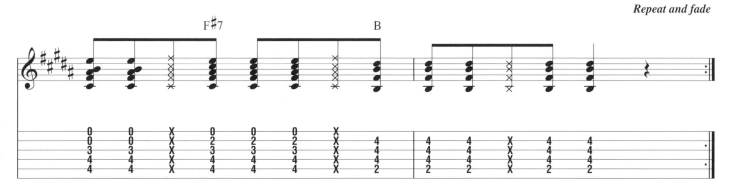

F#7 · B

Take It Easy

Words and Music by Jackson Browne and Glenn Frey

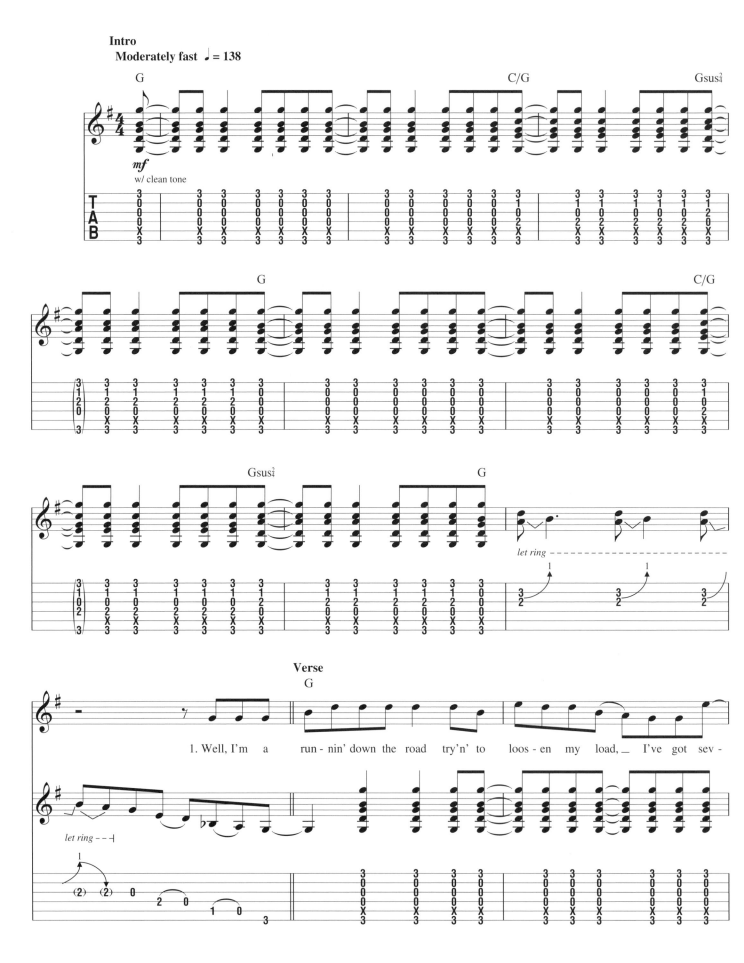

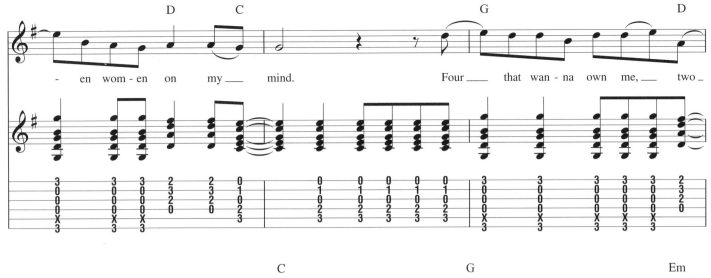

-en wom-en on my __ mind. Four __ that wan-na own me, __ two __

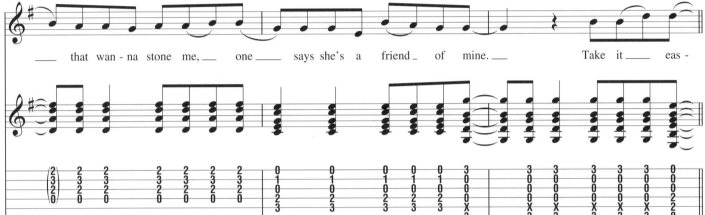

__ that wan-na stone me, __ one __ says she's a friend __ of mine. __ Take it __ eas-

Chorus

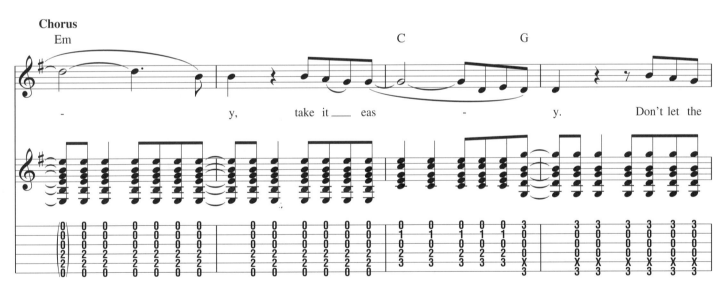

-y, take it __ eas - y. Don't let the

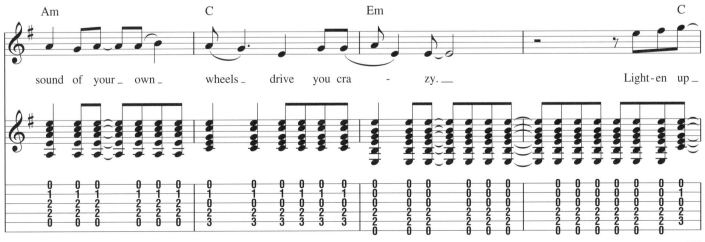

sound of your __ own __ wheels __ drive you cra - zy. __ Light-en up __

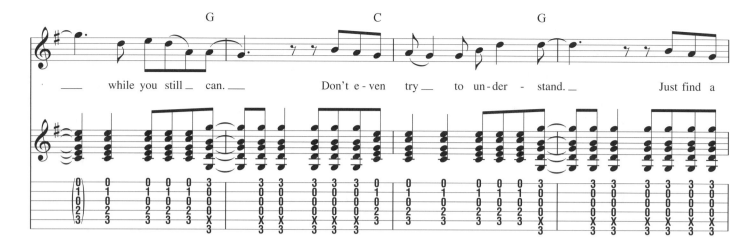

while you still __ can. __ Don't e - ven try __ to un-der - stand. __ Just find a

place to make __ your __ stand __ and take it eas - - - - y. _____

Verse

G

2. Well, I'm a stand-in' on a cor - ner in Win -

D   C

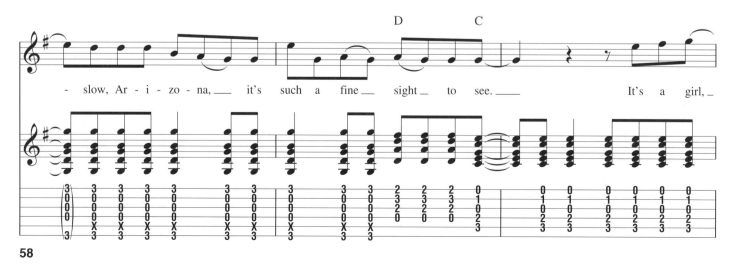

- slow, Ar - i - zo - na, ___ it's such a fine __ sight __ to see. ___ It's a girl, __

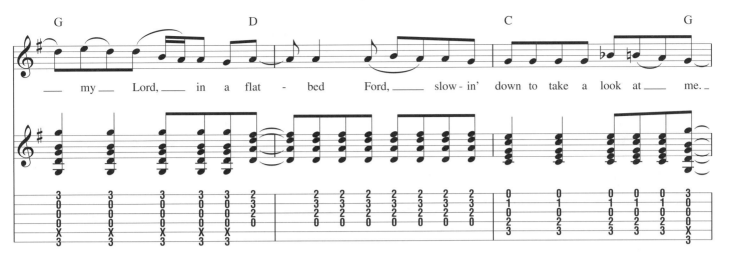

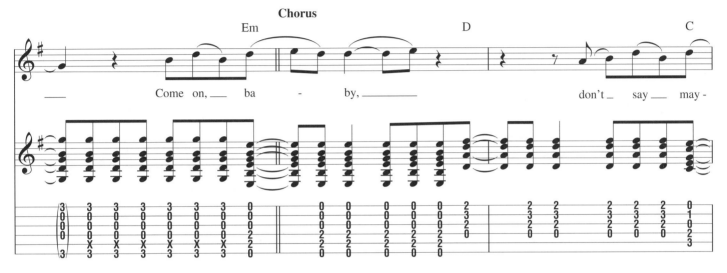

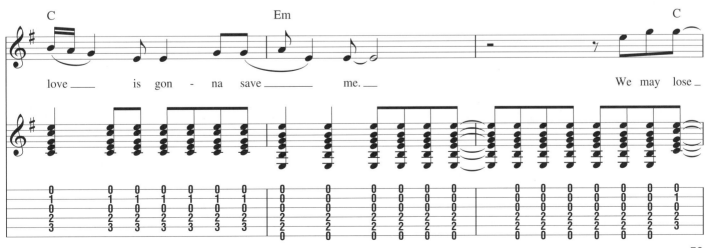

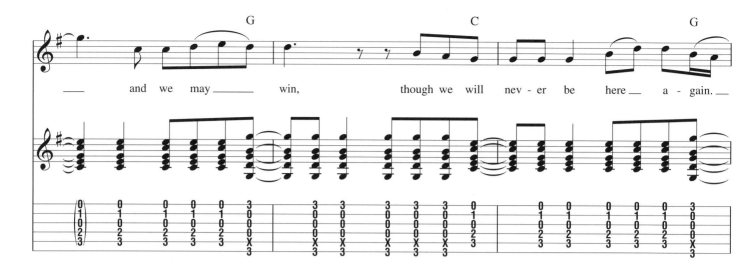

and we may ___ win, though we will nev - er be here ___ a - gain.

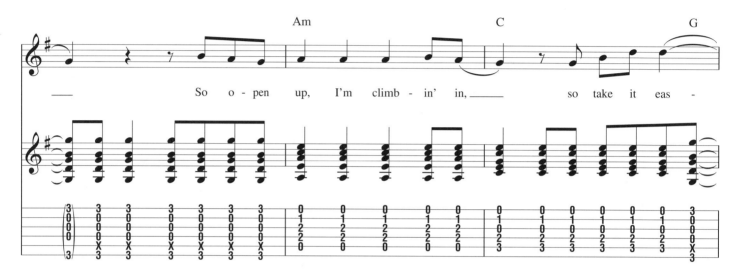

So o - pen up, I'm climb - in' in, ___ so take it eas -

Guitar Solo

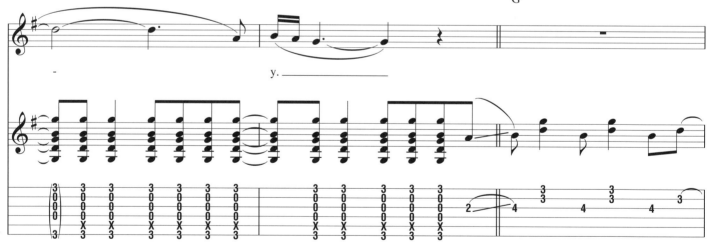

- y. ___

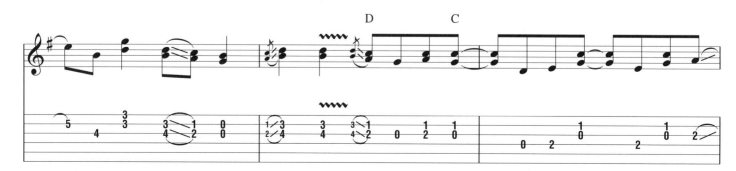

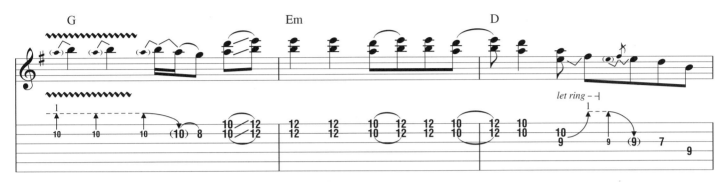

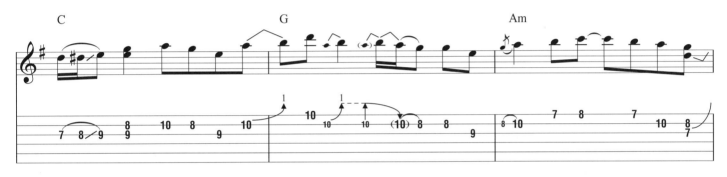

3. Well, I'm a

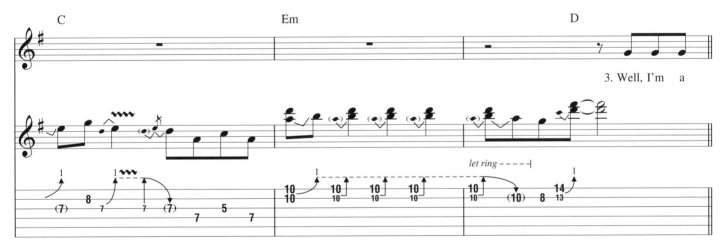

Verse

run - nin' down the road   try'n' to   loos - en my   load, ___ got a   world ___ of trou - ble on   my ___

mind.   Look - in' for a lov - er who won't blow my cov - er; she's

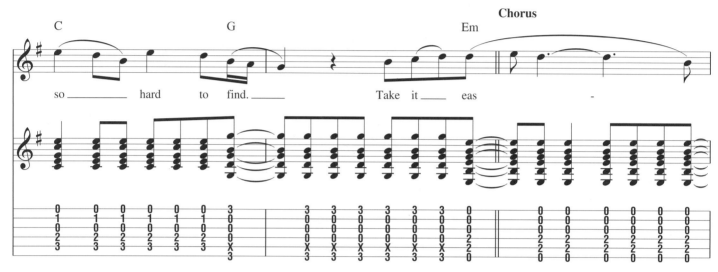

so _____ hard to find. _____ Take it _____ eas -

Chorus

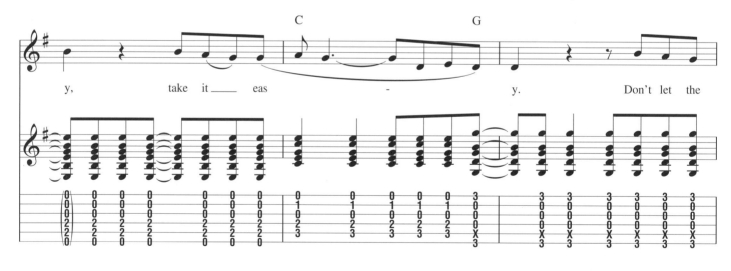

y,   take it _____ eas -   y. Don't let the

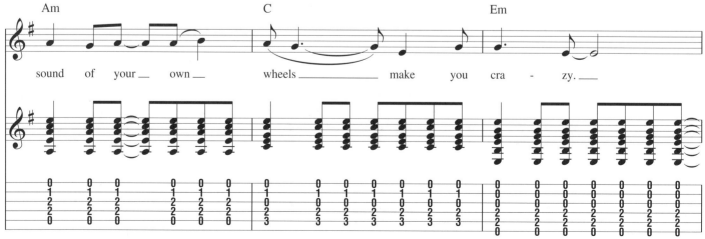

sound of your _ own _ wheels _____ make you cra - zy. ____

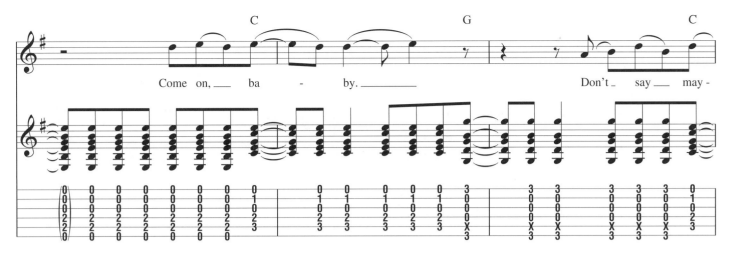

Come on, ____ ba - by. _____ Don't _ say ___ may -

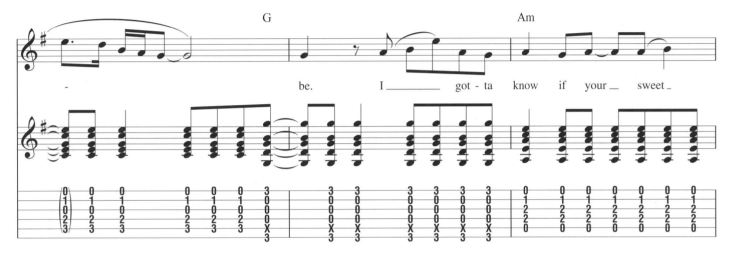

be. I _____ got - ta know if your ___ sweet _

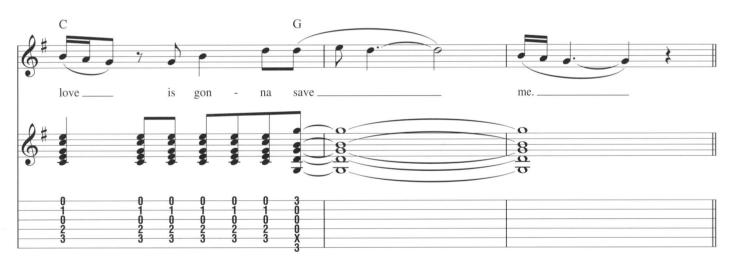

love _____ is gon - na save _____ me.

Outro

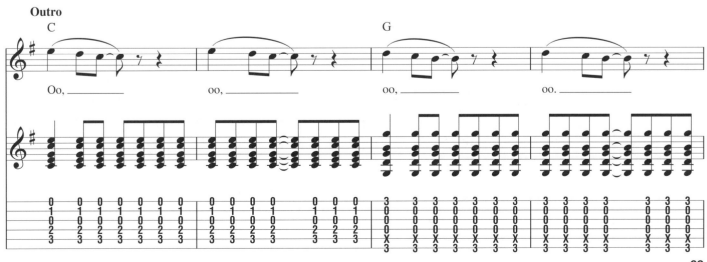

Oo, _____ oo, _____ oo, _____ oo.

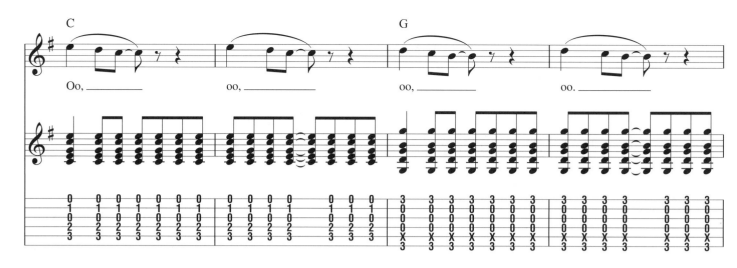

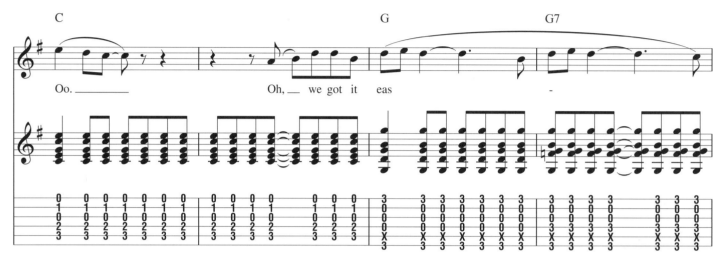

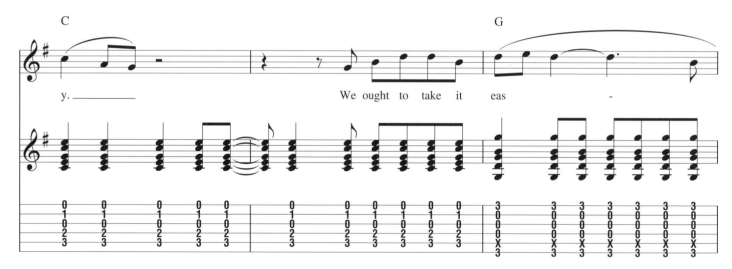

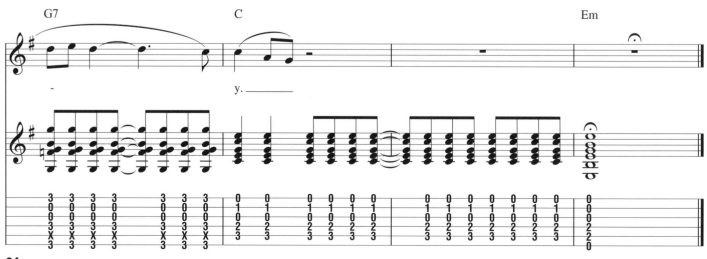

Tequila Sunrise

Words and Music by Don Henley and Glenn Frey

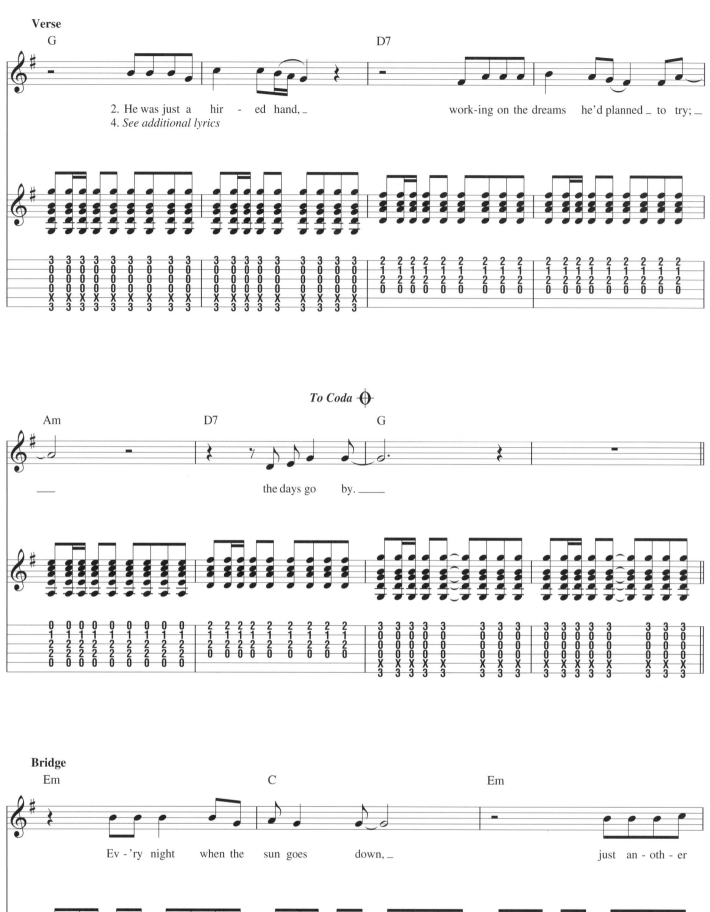

Verse

2. He was just a hir - ed hand, _ work-ing on the dreams he'd planned _ to try; _
4. *See additional lyrics*

To Coda ⊕

the days go by. ____

Bridge

Ev - 'ry night when the sun goes down, _ just an - oth - er

lone - ly boy ___ in town.   And she's out run - nin' 'round. _____

Coda

D.S. al Coda

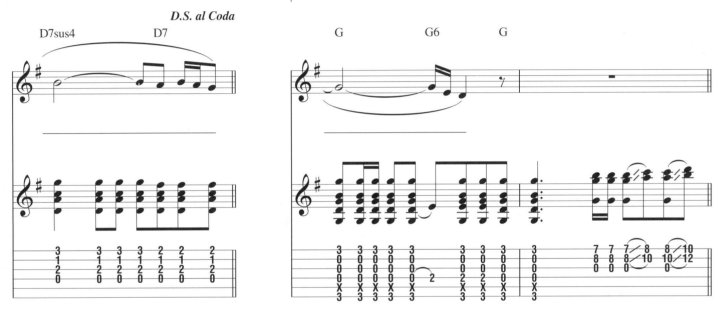

Guitar Solo

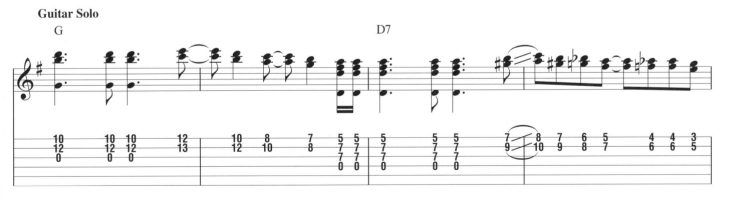

Bridge

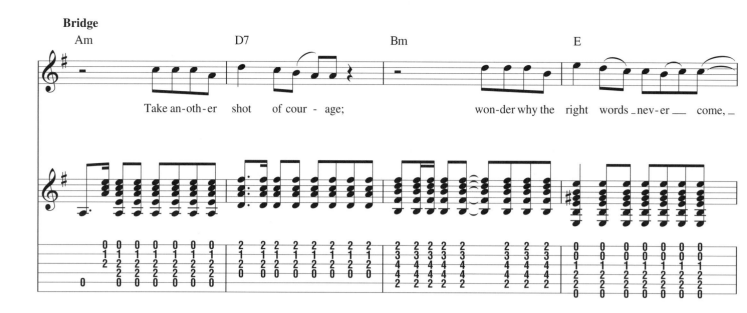

Take an-oth-er shot of cour-age; wonder why the right words _nev-er_ come, _

you just get _ numb. _

Verse

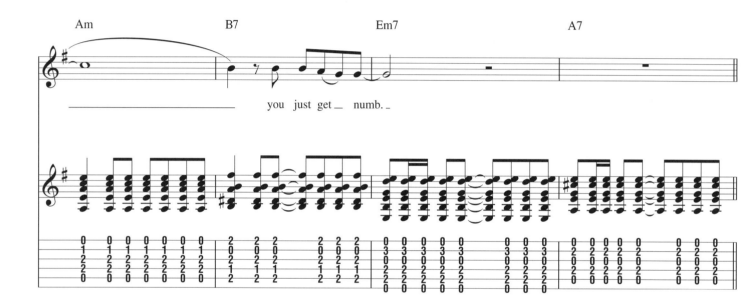

5. It's an-oth-er Te-qui - la Sun - rise; this old world _

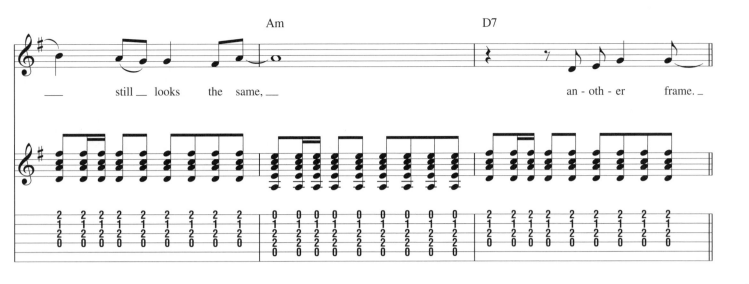

still — looks the same, — an - oth - er frame. —

Outro

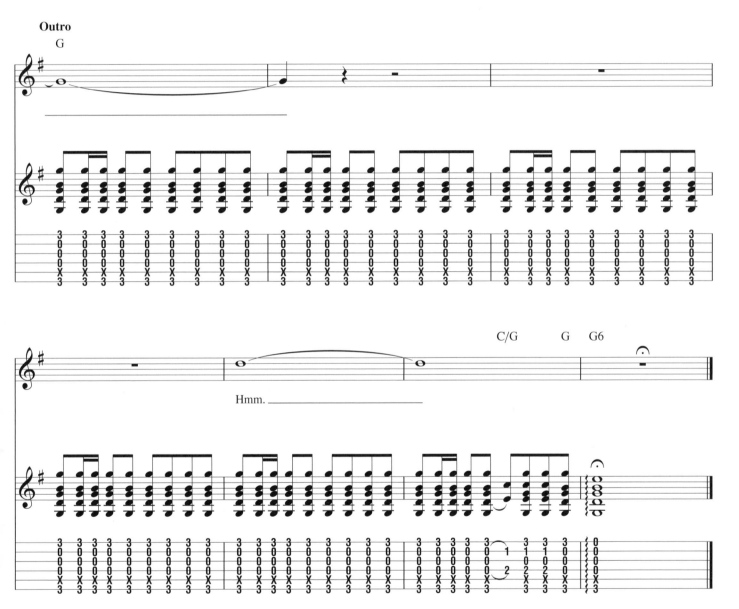

Hmm. —

Additional Lyrics

3. She wasn't just another woman,
   And I couldn't keep from comin' on;
   It's been so long.

4. Whoa, and it's a hollow feelin'
   When it comes down to dealing friends;
   It never ends.

HAL•LEONARD
GUITAR PLAY-ALONG

INCLUDES TAB — AUDIO ACCESS INCLUDED

This series will help you play your favorite songs quickly and easily. Just follow the tab and listen to the audio to hear how the guitar should sound, and then play along using the separate backing tracks.

Playback tools are provided for slowing down the tempo without changing pitch and looping challenging parts. The melody and lyrics are included in the book so that you can sing or simply follow along.

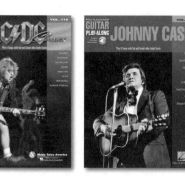

5. LATIN
700939 .... $16.99

6. WEEZER
700958 .... $14.99

7. CREAM
701069 .... $16.99

8. THE WHO
701053 .... $16.99

9. STEVE MILLER
701054 .... $19.99

0. SLIDE GUITAR HITS
701055 .... $16.99

1. JOHN MELLENCAMP
701056 .... $14.99

2. QUEEN
701052 .... $16.99

3. JIM CROCE
701058 .... $17.99

4. BON JOVI
701060 .... $16.99

5. JOHNNY CASH
701070 .... $16.99

6. THE VENTURES
701124 .... $17.99

7. BRAD PAISLEY
701224 .... $16.99

8. ERIC JOHNSON
701353 .... $16.99

9. AC/DC CLASSICS
701356 .... $17.99

0. PROGRESSIVE ROCK
701457 .... $14.99

1. U2
701508 .... $16.99

2. CROSBY, STILLS & NASH
701610 .... $16.99

3. LENNON & McCARTNEY ACOUSTIC
701614 .... $16.99

4. SMOOTH JAZZ
200664 .... $16.99

5. JEFF BECK
701687 .... $17.99

6. BOB MARLEY
701701 .... $17.99

7. 1970S ROCK
701739 .... $16.99

8. 1960S ROCK
701740 .... $14.99

129. MEGADETH
00701741 .... $17.99

130. IRON MAIDEN
00701742 .... $17.99

131. 1990S ROCK
00701743 .... $14.99

132. COUNTRY ROCK
00701757 .... $15.99

133. TAYLOR SWIFT
00701894 .... $16.99

134. AVENGED SEVENFOLD
00701906 .... $16.99

135. MINOR BLUES
00151350 .... $17.99

136. GUITAR THEMES
00701922 .... $14.99

137. IRISH TUNES
00701966 .... $15.99

138. BLUEGRASS CLASSICS
00701967 .... $17.99

139. GARY MOORE
00702370 .... $16.99

140. MORE STEVIE RAY VAUGHAN
00702396 .... $17.99

141. ACOUSTIC HITS
00702401 .... $16.99

142. GEORGE HARRISON
00237697 .... $17.99

143. SLASH
00702425 .... $19.99

144. DJANGO REINHARDT
00702531 .... $16.99

145. DEF LEPPARD
00702532 .... $19.99

146. ROBERT JOHNSON
00702533 .... $16.99

147. SIMON & GARFUNKEL
14041591 .... $16.99

148. BOB DYLAN
14041592 .... $16.99

149. AC/DC HITS
14041593 .... $17.99

150. ZAKK WYLDE
02501717 .... $19.99

151. J.S. BACH
02501730 .... $16.99

152. JOE BONAMASSA
02501751 .... $19.99

153. RED HOT CHILI PEPPERS
00702990 .... $19.99

155. ERIC CLAPTON – FROM THE ALBUM UNPLUGGED
00703085 .... $16.99

156. SLAYER
00703770 .... $19.99

157. FLEETWOOD MAC
00101382 .... $17.99

159. WES MONTGOMERY
00102593 .... $19.99

160. T-BONE WALKER
00102641 .... $17.99

161. THE EAGLES – ACOUSTIC
00102659 .... $17.99

162. THE EAGLES HITS
00102667 .... $17.99

163. PANTERA
00103036 .... $17.99

164. VAN HALEN 1986-1995
00110270 .... $17.99

165. GREEN DAY
00210343 .... $17.99

166. MODERN BLUES
00700764 .... $16.99

167. DREAM THEATER
00111938 .... $24.99

168. KISS
00113421 .... $17.99

169. TAYLOR SWIFT
00115982 .... $16.99

170. THREE DAYS GRACE
00117337 .... $16.99

171. JAMES BROWN
00117420 .... $16.99

172. THE DOOBIE BROTHERS
00116970 .... $16.99

173. TRANS-SIBERIAN ORCHESTRA
00119907 .... $19.99

174. SCORPIONS
00122119 .... $16.99

175. MICHAEL SCHENKER
00122127 .... $17.99

176. BLUES BREAKERS WITH JOHN MAYALL & ERIC CLAPTON
00122132 .... $19.99

177. ALBERT KING
00123271 .... $16.99

178. JASON MRAZ
00124165 .... $17.99

179. RAMONES
00127073 .... $16.99

180. BRUNO MARS
00129706 .... $16.99

181. JACK JOHNSON
00129854 .... $16.99

182. SOUNDGARDEN
00138161 .... $17.99

183. BUDDY GUY
00138240 .... $17.99

184. KENNY WAYNE SHEPHERD
00138258 .... $17.99

185. JOE SATRIANI
00139457 .... $17.99

186. GRATEFUL DEAD
00139459 .... $17.99

187. JOHN DENVER
00140839 .... $17.99

188. MÖTLEY CRUE
00141145 .... $17.99

189. JOHN MAYER
00144350 .... $17.99

190. DEEP PURPLE
00146152 .... $17.99

191. PINK FLOYD CLASSICS
00146164 .... $17.99

192. JUDAS PRIEST
00151352 .... $17.99

193. STEVE VAI
00156028 .... $19.99

194. PEARL JAM
00157925 .... $17.99

195. METALLICA: 1983-1988
00234291 .... $19.99

196. METALLICA: 1991-2016
00234292 .... $19.99

HAL•LEONARD®

For complete songlists, visit
Hal Leonard online at
www.halleonard.com

Prices, contents, and availability subject to
change without notice.

1120
9/12; 397

RECORDED VERSIONS®

The Best Note-For-Note Transcriptions Available

AUTHENTIC TRANSCRIPTIONS WITH NOTES AND TABLATURE

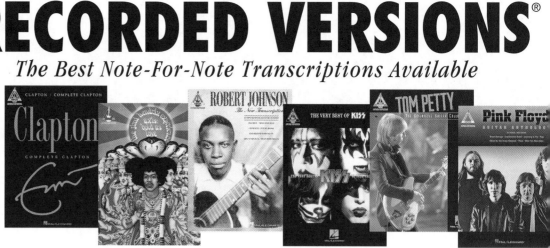

00690603	Aerosmith – O Yeah! Ultimate Hits ...	$27.99
00690178	Alice in Chains – Acoustic	$19.99
00694865	Alice in Chains – Dirt	$19.99
00694925	Alice in Chains – Jar of Flies/Sap.....	$19.99
00691091	Alice Cooper – Best of.....................	$24.99
00690958	Duane Allman – Guitar Anthology	$29.99
00694932	Allman Brothers Band – Volume 1.....	$27.99
00694933	Allman Brothers Band – Volume 2.....	$24.99
00694934	Allman Brothers Band – Volume 3.....	$24.99
00690945	Alter Bridge – Blackbird..................	$24.99
00123558	Arctic Monkeys – AM	$24.99
00214869	Avenged Sevenfold – Best of 2005-2013	$24.99
00690489	Beatles – 1	$24.99
00694929	Beatles – 1962-1966	$24.99
00694930	Beatles – 1967-1970	$27.99
00694880	Beatles – Abbey Road.....................	$19.99
00694832	Beatles – Acoustic Guitar................	$24.99
00690110	Beatles – White Album (Book 1).......	$19.99
00692385	Chuck Berry	$22.99
00147787	Black Crowes – Best of	$19.99
00690149	Black Sabbath	$17.99
00690901	Black Sabbath – Best of..................	$22.99
00691010	Black Sabbath – Heaven and Hell	$22.99
00690148	Black Sabbath – Master of Reality	$17.99
00690142	Black Sabbath – Paranoid	$16.99
00148544	Michael Bloomfield – Guitar Anthology	$24.99
00158600	Joe Bonamassa – Blues of Desperation	$22.99
00198117	Joe Bonamassa – Muddy Wolf at Red Rocks	$24.99
00283540	Joe Bonamassa – Redemption	$24.99
00690913	Boston	$19.99
00690491	David Bowie – Best of.....................	$19.99
00286503	Big Bill Broonzy – Guitar Collection ..	$19.99
00690261	The Carter Family Collection	$19.99
00691079	Johnny Cash – Best of.....................	$22.99
00690936	Eric Clapton – Complete Clapton.......	$29.99
00694869	Eric Clapton – Unplugged	$24.99
00124873	Eric Clapton – Unplugged (Deluxe) ...	$27.99
00138731	Eric Clapton & Friends – The Breeze	$22.99
00139967	Coheed & Cambria – In Keeping Secrets of Silent Earth: 3	$24.99
00141704	Jesse Cook – Works, Vol. 1	$19.99
00288787	Creed – Greatest Hits.....................	$22.99
00690819	Creedence Clearwater Revival	$24.99
00690648	Jim Croce – Very Best of..................	$19.99
00690572	Steve Cropper – Soul Man	$19.99
00690613	Crosby, Stills & Nash – Best of........	$27.99
00690784	Def Leppard – Best of	$22.99
00695831	Derek and the Dominos – Layla & Other Assorted Love Songs ..	$24.99
00291164	Dream Theater – Distance Over Time	$24.99
00278631	Eagles – Greatest Hits 1971-1975	$22.99
00278632	Eagles – Very Best of	$34.99
00690515	Extreme II – Pornograffiti................	$24.99
00150257	John Fahey – Guitar Anthology	$19.99
00690664	Fleetwood Mac – Best of..................	$24.99
00691024	Foo Fighters – Greatest Hits............	$22.99
00120220	Robben Ford – Guitar Anthology	$29.99
00295410	Rory Gallagher – Blues....................	$24.99
00139460	Grateful Dead – Guitar Anthology......	$24.99

00691190	Peter Green – Best of......................	$24.99
00287517	Greta Van Fleet – Anthem of the Peaceful Army	$19.99
00287515	Greta Van Fleet – From the Fires	$19.99
00694798	George Harrison – Anthology...........	$22.99
00692930	Jimi Hendrix – Are You Experienced?	$27.99
00692931	Jimi Hendrix – Axis: Bold As Love.....	$24.99
00690304	Jimi Hendrix – Band of Gypsys	$24.99
00694944	Jimi Hendrix – Blues.......................	$27.99
00692932	Jimi Hendrix – Electric Ladyland.......	$27.99
00660029	Buddy Holly – Best of......................	$22.99
00200446	Iron Maiden – Guitar Tab.................	$29.99
00694912	Eric Johnson – Ah Via Musicom	$24.99
00690271	Robert Johnson – Transcriptions.......	$24.99
00690427	Judas Priest – Best of	$24.99
00690492	B.B. King – Anthology.....................	$24.99
00130447	B.B. King – Live at the Regal	$19.99
00690134	Freddie King – Collection	$19.99
00327968	Marcus King – El Dorado	$22.99
00690157	Kiss – Alive	$19.99
00690356	Kiss – Alive II	$22.99
00291163	Kiss – Very Best of	$22.99
00690377	Kris Kristofferson – Guitar Collection	$19.99
00690834	Lamb of God – Ashes of the Wake	$24.99
00690525	George Lynch – Best of....................	$24.99
00690955	Lynyrd Skynyrd – All-Time Greatest Hits	$24.99
00694954	Lynyrd Skynyrd – New Best of	$24.99
00690577	Yngwie Malmsteen – Anthology	$29.99
00694896	John Mayall with Eric Clapton – Blues Breakers	$19.99
00694952	Megadeth – Countdown to Extinction	$24.99
00276065	Megadeth – Greatest Hits: Back to the Start	$24.99
00694951	Megadeth – Rust in Peace	$24.99
00690011	Megadeth – Youthanasia	$24.99
00209876	Metallica – Hardwired to Self-Destruct	$22.99
00690646	Pat Metheny – One Quiet Night	$22.99
00102591	Wes Montgomery – Guitar Anthology	$24.99
00691092	Gary Moore – Best of	$24.99
00694802	Gary Moore – Still Got the Blues	$24.99
00355456	Alanis Morisette – Jagged Little Pill	$22.99
00690611	Nirvana..	$22.95
00694913	Nirvana – In Utero..........................	$19.99
00694883	Nirvana – Nevermind......................	$19.99
00690026	Nirvana – Unplugged in New York.....	$19.99
00265439	Nothing More – Tab Collection..........	$24.99
00243349	Opeth – Best of..............................	$22.99
00690499	Tom Petty – Definitive Guitar Collection	$19.99
00121933	Pink Floyd – Acoustic Guitar Collection	$24.99
00690428	Pink Floyd – Dark Side of the Moon ..	$19.99
00244637	Pink Floyd – Guitar Anthology	$24.99
00239799	Pink Floyd – The Wall	$24.99
00690789	Poison – Best of.............................	$19.99
00690625	Prince – Very Best of......................	$22.99
00690003	Queen – Classic Queen	$24.99
00694975	Queen – Greatest Hits	$25.99
00694910	Rage Against the Machine................	$22.99
00119834	Rage Against the Machine – Guitar Anthology	$24.99

00690426	Ratt – Best of.................................	$19
00690055	Red Hot Chili Peppers – Blood Sugar Sex Magik.................	$19
00690379	Red Hot Chili Peppers – Californication................................	$19
00690673	Red Hot Chili Peppers – Greatest Hits	$22
00690852	Red Hot Chili Peppers – Stadium Arcadium	$27
00690511	Django Reinhardt – Definitive Collection	$22
00690014	Rolling Stones – Exile on Main Street	$24
00690631	Rolling Stones – Guitar Anthology	$29
00323854	Rush – The Spirit of Radio: Greatest Hits, 1974-1987................	$22
00173534	Santana – Guitar Anthology.............	$27
00276350	Joe Satriani – What Happens Next ...	$24
00690566	Scorpions – Best of........................	$24
00690604	Bob Seger – Guitar Collection	$24
00234543	Ed Sheeran – Divide*.....................	$19
00691114	Slash – Guitar Anthology	$29
00690813	Slayer – Guitar Collection	$19
00690419	Slipknot	$19
00316982	Smashing Pumpkins – Greatest Hits .	$22
00690912	Soundgarden – Guitar Anthology	$24
00120004	Steely Dan – Best of.......................	$24
00120081	Sublime	$19
00690531	System of a Down – Toxicity.............	$19
00694824	James Taylor – Best of....................	$19
00694887	Thin Lizzy – Best of........................	$19
00253237	Trivium – Guitar Tab Anthology........	$24
00690683	Robin Trower – Bridge of Sighs........	$19
00156024	Steve Vai – Guitar Anthology	$34
00660137	Steve Vai – Passion & Warfare	$27
00295076	Van Halen – 30 Classics	$29
00690024	Stevie Ray Vaughan – Couldn't Stand the Weather..............	$19
00660058	Stevie Ray Vaughan – Lightnin' Blues 1983-1987................	$29
00217455	Stevie Ray Vaughan – Plays Slow Blues...........................	$19
00694835	Stevie Ray Vaughan – The Sky Is Crying	$24
00690015	Stevie Ray Vaughan – Texas Flood ...	$19
00694789	Muddy Waters – Deep Blues.............	$24
00152161	Doc Watson – Guitar Anthology........	$22
00690071	Weezer (The Blue Album)................	$19
00117511	Whitesnake – Guitar Collection	$22
00122303	Yes – Guitar Collection	$22
00690443	Frank Zappa – Hot Rats	$22
00121684	ZZ Top – Early Classics...................	$27
00690589	ZZ Top – Guitar Anthology	$24.9

COMPLETE SERIES LIST ONLINE!

HAL•LEONARD

www.halleonard.com

Prices and availability subject to change without notice.
*Tab transcriptions only.

07
2